5.⁰⁰

D0292586

COCKTAILS
2012

FOOD&**WINE**

FOOD & WINE COCKTAILS 2012

EDITOR **Kate Krader**
DEPUTY EDITOR **Jim Meehan**
SENIOR EDITOR **Colleen McKinney**
ASSISTANT EDITOR / TESTER **John deBary**
COPY EDITOR **Lisa Leventer**
RESEARCHER **Matthew Shepatin**
EDITORIAL ASSISTANT **Allison Caruana**

ART DIRECTOR **Courtney Waddell Eckersley**
DESIGNER **Michelle Leong**
PRODUCTION MANAGER **Matt Carson**
FOOD RECIPE TESTER **Justin Chapple**

PHOTOGRAPHER **Lucas Allen**
FOOD STYLIST **Alison Attenborough**
STYLE EDITOR **Jessica Romm**
STYLE ASSISTANT **Suzie Myers**

ON THE COVER **(left)** Margarita, p. 99;
Mexico 70, p. 100

AMERICAN EXPRESS PUBLISHING CORPORATION

PRESIDENT / CEO **Ed Kelly**
CHIEF MARKETING OFFICER & PRESIDENT,
DIGITAL MEDIA **Mark V. Stanich**
SVP / CHIEF FINANCIAL OFFICER **Paul B. Francis**
VPs / GENERAL MANAGERS **Frank Bland,
Keith Strohmeier**

VP, BOOKS & PRODUCTS / PUBLISHER **Marshall Corey**
DIRECTOR, BOOK PROGRAMS **Bruce Spanier**
SENIOR MARKETING MANAGER, BRANDED BOOKS
Eric Lucie
ASSISTANT MARKETING MANAGER **Stacy Mallis**
DIRECTOR OF FULFILLMENT & PREMIUM VALUE
Philip Black
MANAGER OF CUSTOMER EXPERIENCE
& PRODUCT DEVELOPMENT **Charles Graver**
DIRECTOR OF FINANCE **Thomas Noonan**
ASSOCIATE BUSINESS MANAGER **Uma Mahabir**
OPERATIONS DIRECTOR (PREPRESS)
Rosalie Abatemarco Samat
OPERATIONS DIRECTOR (MANUFACTURING)
Anthony White

ISBN 978-1-932624-43-4
ISSN 1554-4354

Published by American Express Publishing Corporation
1120 Avenue of the Americas, New York, New York 10036

Manufactured in the United States of America

FOOD & WINE MAGAZINE

SVP / EDITOR IN CHIEF **Dana Cowin**
CREATIVE DIRECTOR **Stephen Scoble**
MANAGING EDITOR **Mary Ellen Ward**
EXECUTIVE EDITOR **Pamela Kaufman**
EXECUTIVE FOOD EDITOR **Tina Ujlaki**
EXECUTIVE WINE EDITOR **Ray Isle**
EXECUTIVE DIGITAL EDITOR **Rebecca Bauer**
DEPUTY EDITOR **Christine Quinlan**

FEATURES
FEATURES EDITOR **Michael Endelman**
RESTAURANT EDITOR **Kate Krader**
TRAVEL EDITOR **Gina Hamadey**
STYLE EDITOR **Jessica Romm**
ASSOCIATE WINE EDITOR **Megan Krigbaum**
EDITORIAL ASSISTANTS **Maren Ellingboe,
Chelsea Morse, M. Elizabeth Sheldon**

FOOD
DEPUTY EDITOR **Kate Heddings**
SENIOR EDITOR **Kristin Donnelly**
ASSOCIATE EDITOR **Daniel Gritzer**
TEST KITCHEN SUPERVISOR **Marcia Kiesel**
SENIOR RECIPE DEVELOPER **Grace Parisi**
ASSISTANT RECIPE TESTER **Justin Chapple**
EDITORIAL ASSISTANT **Maggie Mariolis**
TEST KITCHEN ASSISTANT **Gina Mungiovi**

ART
ART DIRECTOR **Courtney Waddell Eckersley**
SENIOR DESIGNERS **James Maikowski,
Michael Patti**
BOOK DESIGNER **Michelle Leong**
DIGITAL DESIGNER **Jonathan Moran**

PHOTO
DIRECTOR OF PHOTOGRAPHY **Fredrika Stjärne**
DEPUTY PHOTO EDITOR **Anthony LaSala**
ASSOCIATE PHOTO EDITOR **Sara Parks**
PHOTO ASSISTANT **Tomi Omololu-Lange**

PRODUCTION
PRODUCTION DIRECTOR **M. Cristina Martinez**
PRODUCTION MANAGER **Matt Carson**
PRODUCTION ASSISTANT **Amelia Grohman**

COPY & RESEARCH
COPY DIRECTOR **Michele Berkover Petry**
SENIOR COPY EDITOR **Ann Lien**
ASSISTANT RESEARCH EDITOR **Erin Laverty**

DIGITAL MEDIA
DESIGN DIRECTOR **Patricia Sanchez**
FEATURES EDITOR **Alex Vallis**
SENIOR EDITOR **Lawrence Marcus**
ASSOCIATE EDITOR **Alessandra Bulow**
ASSISTANT EDITOR **Justine Sterling**
ASSOCIATE ART DIRECTOR **Jooyoung Hsu**
EDITORIAL PROJECT COORDINATOR
Kerianne Hansen
EDITORIAL ASSISTANT **Jasmin Sun**

F&W
COCKTAILS
2012

FOOD&**WINE**
BOOKS

American Express Publishing Corporation, New York

Left to right: "Mitos" coupe from Ameico; "Basso" coupe by Calvin Klein; "Circus" wallpaper by Cole & Son.

STEVE MCQUEEN P.152

BONDAGE P.152

CONTENTS

"Optic" tumbler by Ciovere.

MOJITO P.110

FOREWORD

Everyone loves a classic cocktail—from old-school bartenders to trend-obsessed mixologists to customers who adore those drinks. Now cocktail innovators are taking the classics as a starting point and using their improvisational skills to create new drinks that we believe are destined to be the next classics. Here are 44 iconic cocktails—from the legendary Manhattan, created in the late 1800s, to the much-maligned Cosmopolitan, popular in the 1990s—and over 100 excellent updates. We've also chronicled the latest mixology trends (like smoky drinks), sought out some of the nation's most cocktail-friendly bar food and compiled a tools and glassware section that reflects bartenders' ever-evolving arsenals. If you prefer to go out for drinks rather than make them, check out our list of 100 of America's best drinking spots. Feel free to challenge bartenders there to make you a terrific drink—classic or creative.

Dana Cowin
Editor in Chief
FOOD & WINE Magazine

Jim Meehan
Deputy Editor
FOOD & WINE Cocktails 2012

GLASSWARE

1 MARTINI
A stemmed glass with a cone-shaped bowl for cocktails that are served straight up (drinks that are mixed with ice and then strained).

2 ROCKS
A short, wide-mouthed glass for spirits served neat (without ice) and cocktails poured over ice. **SINGLE ROCKS** glasses hold up to 6 ounces; **DOUBLE ROCKS** glasses hold closer to 12.

3 COLLINS
A very tall, narrow glass often used for drinks that are served on ice and topped with soda.

4 WINEGLASS
A tall, slightly rounded, stemmed glass for wine-based cocktails. White wine glasses are a fine substitute for highball glasses and are also good for frozen drinks. Balloon-shaped red wine glasses are ideal for fruity cocktails as well as for punches.

5 HIGHBALL
A tall, narrow glass that helps preserve the fizz in drinks served with ice and topped with club soda or tonic water.

6 COUPE
A shallow, wide-mouthed glass primarily for small (short) and potent cocktails.

7 PILSNER
A flared glass designed for beer. It's also good for serving oversize cocktails or drinks with multiple garnishes.

8 HEATPROOF MUG
A durable ceramic or glass cup with a handle. Perfect for coffee spiked with whiskey or other spirits as well as for assorted hot drinks.

9 FLUTE
A tall, slender, usually stemmed glass; its narrow shape helps keep cocktails topped with Champagne or sparkling wine effervescent.

10 FIZZ
A narrow glass for soda-topped drinks without ice. Also called a Delmonico or juice glass.

HOME BAR TOOLS

1 ICE PICK

A sharp metal tool with a sturdy handle used to break off chunks from a larger block of ice.

2 BAR SPOON

A long-handled metal spoon that mixes cocktails without creating air bubbles. Also useful to measure small amounts.

3 Y PEELER

A wide peeler that's great for making large and small twists from citrus-fruit peels.

4 JULEP STRAINER

The preferred device for straining cocktails from a pint glass because it fits securely. Fine holes keep ice out of the drink.

5 WAITER'S CORKSCREW

A pocketknife-like tool with a bottle opener. Bartenders favor it over bulkier, more complicated corkscrews.

6 COBBLER SHAKER

The most commonly used shaker, with a metal cup for mixing drinks with ice, a built-in strainer and a fitted top.

7 ATOMIZER

A small spray bottle used to coat an empty glass with aromatic liquid, such as absinthe, instead of rinsing the glass. Atomizers are sold at beauty supply stores.

8 HAWTHORNE STRAINER

The best all-purpose strainer. A semicircular spring ensures a spill-proof fit on a shaker. Look for a tightly coiled spring, which keeps muddled fruit and herbs out of drinks.

9 CITRUS JUICER

A metal or ceramic press that allows you to squeeze citrus fruit when you need it.

10 BOSTON SHAKER

The bartender's choice; consists of a mixing glass, usually a pint glass, with a metal canister that covers the glass to create a seal. Shake drinks with the metal half pointing away from you.

11 JAPANESE MIXING GLASS

A heavy, often etched glass that's used for stirring. Its spout makes for graceful pouring.

12 JIGGER

A two-sided stainless measuring instrument for precise mixing.

13 MICROPLANE

A fine-toothed metal grater used for shaving citrus zest and ginger. Small box graters are best for hard spices like nutmeg and cinnamon.

14 MUDDLER

A sturdy tool for crushing herbs and fresh fruit; it's traditionally made of wood. Choose a muddler that can reach the bottom of a shaker; in a pinch, use a long-handled wooden spoon.

15 FINE STRAINER

A fine-mesh strainer set over a glass before the cocktail is poured in (see Fine-Straining Drinks on **P.18**). It keeps bits of muddled herbs, fruit and crushed ice out of drinks.

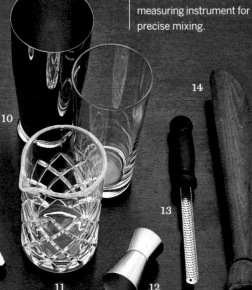

ESSENTIAL SPIRITS

Mixologists are using more and more esoteric spirits in their drinks, but these five choices are still the backbone of a great cocktail list.

GIN

Gin is made by distilling a neutral grain spirit with botanicals such as juniper and dried citrus peel, which often add piney, spicy or citrusy notes. Classic dry gin, the most common type, is also known as **LONDON DRY.** It's bolder in flavor than the slightly sweet, less botanically intense **OLD TOM** style. Distilled with sweet orange peel, **PLYMOUTH GIN** tastes sweeter than London dry. The unofficial gin of the British Royal Navy for nearly two centuries, Plymouth may be produced in just one place: Plymouth, England.

VODKA

Produced all over the world, vodka is traditionally distilled from fermented grain or potatoes, but nearly any fruit or vegetable that contains starch or sugar can be used, from grapes to beets. The finest flavored vodkas are often made with fruit-infused grain alcohol that's then run through a pot still.

TEQUILA

The best examples of this agave-based spirit are made with 100 percent blue agave. **BLANCO** tequila is commonly unaged. **REPOSADO** ("rested") tequila will sit for up to one year. **AÑEJO** ("aged") tequila is aged for up to three years. **MEZCAL,** also agave-based, has a smoky flavor that comes from roasting agave hearts in earthen pits before fermentation. The finest mezcal is made in Mexico's Oaxaca region.

WHISKEY

This spirit is distilled from a fermented mash of grains and aged in wood barrels. (Whiskey is spelled without an "e" in Scotland, Canada and Japan.) **BOURBON,** which tastes of brown sugar and toffee, is distilled primarily from corn. **RYE** whiskey, which is made with a minimum of 51 percent rye, is more grassy. **SCOTCH** is made in two major styles: **single malts,** produced from 100 percent malted barley from one distillery; and **blends,** a mixture of single-malt and grain whisky from more than one distillery.

RUM

Distilled from cane syrup, molasses or fresh pressed sugarcane, rums are primarily produced in tropical regions. **WHITE,** a.k.a. silver or light, rums typically age for a short time in wood. **AMBER,** or gold, rums usually age in oak barrels for at least three years. **DARK** rums, especially Jamaican ones, tend to be rich and flavorful. They often age for five to seven years or more. **RHUM AGRICOLE** is made in the French West Indies from fresh pressed sugarcane juice (not syrup or molasses).

BAR LEXICON

ABSINTHE An herbal, anise-flavored spirit formerly banned in the US. It's flavored with such botanicals as wormwood, green anise and fennel seeds.

AGAVE NECTAR A rich, sweet syrup made from the sap of the cactus-like agave plant.

ALLSPICE DRAM Also known as pimento dram; a rum-based liqueur infused with Jamaican allspice berries. **St. Elizabeth** and **The Bitter Truth** are good brands.

AMARO A bittersweet herbal Italian liqueur often served as an after-dinner drink. There are dozens of brands of amari; both **Averna** and **Amaro Nonino** are widely available in the United States.

APEROL A vibrant red, low-proof Italian aperitif flavored with bitter orange, rhubarb, gentian and cinchona bark.

APPLE BRANDY A distilled fermented cider that is aged in oak barrels. Most apple brandy is bottled at 80 proof, but **bonded** apple

brandy, which is preferable in cocktails because of its concentrated green-apple flavor, is 100 proof. See also **CALVADOS.**

AQUAVIT A clear, grain- or potato-based Scandinavian spirit flavored with caraway seeds and other botanicals, such as fennel, anise and citrus peel.

BÉNÉDICTINE A brandy-based herbal liqueur derived from a recipe developed by a French monk in 1510.

BITTERS A concentrated tincture of bitter and aromatic herbs, roots and spices that adds complexity to drinks. Varieties include orange, grapefruit, cherry and aromatic bitters, the best known of which is **Angostura,** created in 1824. Germany's **Bitter Truth** makes bitters in traditional flavors as well as unusual ones like celery and chocolate. **Fee Brothers** bitters come in 15 flavors and have been made in Rochester, NY, since Prohibition. **Peychaud's** bitters have flavors of anise and cranberry; the recipe dates to 19th-century New Orleans.

BONDED WHISKEY
A whiskey that's been produced by a single distillery, distilled during a single season, aged a minimum of four years, bottled at 100 proof and stored in a "bonded" warehouse under US government supervision.

CACHAÇA A potent Brazilian spirit that's distilled from fermented sugarcane juice.

CALVADOS A cask-aged brandy made in the Normandy region of France from apples and sometimes pears.

CAMPARI A potent, bright red Italian aperitif with a bitter orange flavor. It's made from fruit, herbs and spices.

CARPANO ANTICA FORMULA A rich and complex crimson-colored sweet Italian vermouth.

CHARTREUSE A spicy herbal French liqueur made from more than 100 botanicals; **green** Chartreuse is more potent than the honey-sweetened **yellow** one.

COCCHI AMERICANO A low-alcohol, wine-based aperitif infused with citrus, herbs such as gentian and quinine-rich cinchona bark.

COGNAC An oak-aged brandy made from grapes grown in France's Charente region. **VSOP** (Very Superior Old Pale)

Cognac must be aged a minimum of four years in French oak barrels.

COINTREAU A French triple sec that is made by macerating and distilling sun-dried sweet and bitter orange peels.

CURAÇAO A general term for orange-flavored liqueurs produced in the French West Indies.

CYNAR A pleasantly bitter Italian liqueur made from 13 herbs and plants, including artichokes.

DRAMBUIE A whisky-based Scottish liqueur flavored with honey, herbs and spices.

EAU-DE-VIE A clear, unaged brandy made from fruit. Classic varieties include **framboise** (raspberry), **poire** (pear), **abricot** (apricot), **kirsch** (cherry) and **mirabelle** (plum).

FERNET-BRANCA A potent, bitter-flavored Italian digestif that's made from 27 herbs.

GENEVER A botanically rich, clear, malted grain–based spirit from Holland. **Oude** refers to the maltier old style; lighter, less malty versions are called **jonge.**

GRENADINE A sweet red syrup made from a mix of pomegranate juice and sugar (see the Homemade Grenadine recipe on **P.19**).

GUM SYRUP A simple syrup that's been thickened with gum arabic, a natural gum made from the sap of acacia trees.

HEERING CHERRY LIQUEUR A crimson-colored, brandy-based cherry liqueur made in Denmark since 1818.

KIRSCH Short for *kirschwasser;* an unaged brandy or eau-de-vie produced by pot-stilling crushed morello cherries and their pits.

LICOR 43 A citrus-and-vanilla-flavored Spanish liqueur made from a combination of 43 herbs and spices.

LILLET A wine-based French aperitif flavored with orange peel and quinine. The lesser-known **rouge** variety is sweeter than the more widely available **blanc.**

LIMONCELLO An intensely flavored Italian liqueur made from lemon zest soaked in neutral spirits, then sweetened with sugar.

MARASCHINO LIQUEUR A colorless Italian liqueur. The best brands are distilled from sour marasca cherries and their pits, then aged in ash barrels and sweetened with sugar.

ORGEAT A sweet, non-alcoholic syrup made from almonds or almond extract, sugar and rose or orange flower water.

PIMM'S NO. 1 A gin-based English aperitif often served with ginger beer or lemonade.

PISCO A clear brandy that is distilled from grapes in the wine-producing regions of Peru and Chile.

PORT A fortified wine from the Douro region of Portugal. Styles include fruity, young **ruby** port; richer, nuttier **tawny;** thick-textured, oak-aged **late bottled vintage (LBV);** and decadent **vintage** port, made from the best grapes in the best vintages. Dry **white** port is often served chilled, as an aperitif.

ROOT LIQUEUR A sugar-cane-distilled liqueur flavored with birch bark, smoked black tea, citrus peels, cloves and other spices. Art in the Age, in Philadelphia, is the main producer.

SHERRY A fortified wine from Spain's Jerez region. Varieties include dry styles like **fino** and **manzanilla;** nuttier, richer **amontillado** and **oloroso;** and viscous, sweet **Pedro Ximénez (PX)** and **cream** sherry. **East India** sherry falls between an oloroso and a PX in style.

SHOCHU A Japanese vodka-like spirit distilled from a variety of ingredients, such as rice, buckwheat or barley.

ST-GERMAIN ELDER-FLOWER LIQUEUR A French liqueur made by blending macerated elderflower blossoms with eau-de-vie. It has hints of pear, peach and grapefruit zest.

STREGA An Italian liqueur infused with approximately 70 herbs and spices. One of them is saffron, which gives it a golden yellow color.

TRIPLE SEC An orange-flavored liqueur that is similar to curaçao but not as sweet. **Cointreau,** created in 1875, is the most famous. **Combier,** created in 1834, claims to be the world's first.

VERMOUTH An aromatic fortified wine. **Dry** vermouth is used in martinis. The **sweet** variety, which is usually red, is often used to make Manhattans. **Bianco,** or **blanc,** vermouth is a sweet white aromatic vermouth traditionally served on the rocks. **Rosé,** or **rosato,** vermouth is pink, with a spicy flavor.

MIXOLOGY BASICS

MAKING A TWIST

A twist—a small piece of citrus zest—lends a drink concentrated citrus flavor from the peel's essential oils.

TO MAKE AND USE A STANDARD TWIST
1. Use a sharp paring knife or Y peeler to cut a thin, oval, quarter-size disk of the peel, avoiding the pith.
2. Grasp the outer edges skin side down and pinch the twist over the drink. Rub it around the glass rim, then drop it in.

FLAMING A TWIST

Flaming a lemon or orange twist caramelizes the zest's essential oils.
1. Cut a thin, oval, quarter-size piece of peel with a bit of the pith intact.
2. Gently grasp the outer edges skin side down between the thumb and two fingers and hold the twist about 4 inches over the cocktail.
3. Hold a lit match over the drink an inch away from the twist—don't let the flame touch the peel—then pinch the edges of the twist sharply so that the citrus oil falls through the flame and into the drink.

SMACKING HERBS

To accentuate the aroma of fresh herbs used for garnish, clap them between your hands over the glass to release the essential oils into the drink.

FINE-STRAINING DRINKS

Drinks made with muddled fruit or herbs are often double-strained to remove tiny particles, so the cocktail is crystal clear.
1. Set a fine strainer over a serving glass.
2. Prepare the drink in a shaker or pint glass. Set a Hawthorne or julep strainer on top, then pour the drink through both strainers into the serving glass.

PERFECTING ICE

The right ice is essential to preparing a balanced and attractive drink.

TO MAKE BIG BLOCKS OF ICE FOR PUNCH BOWLS, pour water into a large, shallow plastic container and freeze. To unmold, first warm the bottom of the container in hot water.

TO MAKE CRUSHED ICE, cover cubes in a clean kitchen towel and pound with a wooden mallet or rolling pin.

TO MAKE CRACKED ICE, hold an ice cube in your hand; tap it with the back of a bar spoon so it breaks into pieces.

TO MAKE CLEAR CUBES, fill ice trays with hot filtered water.

TO MAKE PERFECTLY SQUARE CUBES, use flexible silicone Perfect Cube ice trays (available at *surlatable.com*).

HOMEMADE MIXERS

SIMPLE SYRUP
MAKES ABOUT 12 OUNCES

In a small saucepan, combine 8 ounces water and 1 cup sugar. Bring to a boil over moderately high heat, stirring until the sugar dissolves, about 3 minutes. Remove from the heat and let cool. Transfer the syrup to a bottle or tightly covered glass jar and refrigerate for up to 1 month.

RICH SIMPLE SYRUP
MAKES ABOUT 8 OUNCES

In a small saucepan, combine 4 ounces water and 1 cup Demerara or other raw sugar. Bring to a boil over moderately high heat, stirring until the sugar dissolves, about 3 minutes. Remove from the heat and let cool. Transfer the syrup to a bottle or tightly covered glass jar and refrigerate for up to 1 month.

EASIEST SIMPLE SYRUP
MAKES ABOUT 12 OUNCES

In a bottle or jar with a tight-fitting lid, shake 8 ounces hot water with 1 cup superfine sugar until the sugar dissolves. Let cool, then refrigerate the syrup for up to 1 month.

A WORD ON HONEY & AGAVE

Natural sweeteners like honey and agave nectar impart a more complex flavor than simple syrup (see Classic Sweeteners, **P.20**). To make a pourable syrup, mix two parts warm honey or agave nectar with one part water. (For a less rich syrup, use a 1:1 ratio.) Or simply shake the sweetener and hot water in a jar. Let the syrup cool before using.

HOMEMADE GRENADINE
MAKES ABOUT 12 OUNCES

In a bottle or jar with a tight-fitting lid, shake 8 ounces unsweetened pomegranate juice with 1 cup sugar until the sugar dissolves. If desired, add ⅛ teaspoon orange flower water. Refrigerate the grenadine for up to 2 weeks.

TRENDS

Smoky flavors and natural sweeteners are invigorating the cocktail world.

amari

Amari and other bittersweet Italian liqueurs are everywhere. They anchor both modern drinks and classics like the Negroni; they've also become popular shots among bartenders. Bars like Amor y Amargo in Manhattan's East Village are even making their own amari.

fine-straining

After so many years of shaking Martinis and pouring them through Hawthorne strainers (so the drink is topped with a layer of tiny ice chips), bartenders are shaking just as hard but have begun straining out *all* the ice to make crystal-clear cocktails. This method is also being used for drinks that are made with muddled herbs and fruit; all bits are strained out but the flavor remains. (See Fine-Straining Drinks on **P.18.**)

classic sweeteners

Mixologists are replacing ubiquitous simple syrup with more complex sweeteners that recall cocktails' early days. Honey, maple syrup, raw sugar, orgeat and grenadine, which bartenders used in the late 1800s, are back, joined by the relative newcomer agave syrup.

extreme locavore cocktails

The intense local-and-sustainable eating movement has taken increasing hold of the cocktail world. Bartenders are relying more on close-to-home purveyors for all of their ingredients—not just produce but also regionally produced spirits, bitters and syrups. This doesn't seem to bother bartenders; it gives their drinks locavore cred.

smoke

For those of you keeping track since F&W's first cocktail book in 2005, the prevailing trend at the time was strong, sweet and sour drinks. Then bitter (as in aromatic bitters) joined the flavor profile, followed by herbal, floral (St-Germain elderflower liqueur) and spicy (chiles, hot sauce). This year's flavor is smoke. Bartenders are mixing drinks with heavily peated Islay malts, mezcal produced from fire pit–roasted agave and smoked ingredients like chipotle chiles, smoked salt and the Baco-Stura Bitters on **P.118.**

CONVERSION CHART

CUP	OUNCE	TBSP	TSP	ML*
4¼ c	34 fl oz			1000 ml
4 c	32 fl oz			950 ml
3 c	24 fl oz			710 ml
2 c	16 fl oz			475 ml
1 c	8 fl oz			240 ml
¾ c	6 fl oz			175 ml
⅔ c	5⅓ fl oz			160 ml
	5 fl oz	10 tbsp		150 ml
½ c	4 fl oz			120 ml
	3 fl oz	6 tbsp		90 ml
⅓ c	2⅔ fl oz			80 ml
¼ c	2 fl oz			60 ml
	1 fl oz	2 tbsp		30 ml
	½ fl oz	1 tbsp	3 tsp	15 ml
	⅓ fl oz	⅔ tbsp	2 tsp	10 ml
	¼ fl oz	½ tbsp	1½ tsp	7 ml

* Conversions to milliliters are approximate.

AMERICANO

Francesco Lafranconi · Southern Wine & Spirits of America · Las Vegas

AMERICANO P.24

Left to right: "Pure" glass by Schott Zwiesel from Fortessa; "Carat" tumbler by Orrefors; "Le Méticuleux" glass by Saint-Louis; "Presidio" cocktail pick from Williams-Sonoma; "Circus" wallpaper by Cole & Son.

SIMPATICO P.25

QUO VADIS P.25

A
B
C
D
E
F
G
H
I
J
K
L
M
N
O
P
Q
R
S
T
U
V
W
X
Y
Z

the classic
■ AMERICANO

This drink was a favorite of American expats during Prohibition. Prior to then it was known as the Milano-Torino, for the cities where its two main ingredients were first made: Milan (Campari) and Turin (sweet vermouth).

◇ **Ice**
◇ **1½ ounces Campari**
◇ **1½ ounces sweet vermouth**
◇ **3 ounces chilled club soda**
◇ **1 orange wheel and 1 lemon twist, for garnish**

◇ Fill a chilled rocks glass with ice. Add the Campari, sweet vermouth and club soda and stir well. Garnish with the orange wheel and lemon twist.

the twist
■ TRECICLO

Francesco Lafranconi swaps in Brachetto, a sweet fizzy red wine, for the Americano's club soda to make his Treciclo (pronounced treh-CHEE-kloh). Garnishing the drink with a slightly tart grapefruit twist and sliced strawberry gives it surprising complexity.

◇ **Ice**
◇ **2 ounces chilled sparkling red wine**
◇ **1 ounce Campari**
◇ **1 ounce sweet vermouth**
◇ **1 grapefruit twist and 1 sliced strawberry, for garnish**

◇ Fill a chilled rocks glass with ice. Add the sparkling red wine, Campari and vermouth and stir well. Garnish with the grapefruit twist and sliced strawberry.

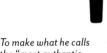

the reinvention

QUO VADIS

Lafranconi teaches mixology seminars on amari, bitter Italian digestive liqueurs. (There are scores of amari, mostly made from secret combinations of herbs and spices.) He chose Amaro Abano for this drink because its cardamom flavor goes so nicely with the rich, nutty cream sherry.

Ice

1 ounce Campari

1 ounce cream sherry, preferably Lustau Rare Cream

½ ounce Luxardo Amaro Abano or other amaro, such as Averna or Amaro Lucano

2 ounces chilled club soda

2 orange twists skewered on a pick with 2 green olives, for garnish

Fill a chilled rocks glass with ice. Add all of the remaining ingredients except the garnish and stir well. Garnish with the skewered orange twists and green olives.

the mocktail

SIMPATICO

To make what he calls the "most authentic alcohol-free replica of an Americano," Lafranconi mixes citrus juices with two nonalcoholic beverages. Italian Sanbittèr soda stands in for Campari; Terma Amargo Serrano, an intensely herbal concoction from Argentina, mimics vermouth. The celery bitters in the drink are alcohol-based; they can be left out of the drink.

Ice

1 grapefruit wedge

1 orange wedge

1 chilled 3.4-ounce bottle Sanbittèr (see Note)

1½ ounces chilled Terma Amargo Serrano (see Note)

Dash of celery bitters (optional)

1 thyme sprig and 1 lemon twist, for garnish

Fill a chilled collins glass with ice. Squeeze the grapefruit and orange wedges into the glass, then drop them in. Add the Sanbittèr, Terma Amargo Serrano and bitters and stir well. Garnish with the thyme sprig and lemon twist.

NOTE Sanbittèr soda is sold at Italian markets. Terma Amargo Serrano is available at *gauchogourmet.com* and at Latin markets.

APEROL SPRITZ

Vincenzo Marianella · Copa d'Oro · Santa Monica, CA

the classic
APEROL SPRITZ

This sparkling cocktail comes from Italy's Veneto region, which is also where Prosecco is made and near where Vincenzo Marianella was born. "This drink was almost mandatory before dinner when I was living in Italy no matter what season it was," he says.

Ice

3 ounces chilled Prosecco

1½ ounces Aperol (bitter orange Italian aperitif)

3 ounces chilled club soda

1 orange slice, for garnish

Fill a large chilled wineglass with ice. Add the Prosecco, Aperol and club soda and stir once or twice. Garnish the drink with the orange slice.

the twist
TERRAZZA

Bittersweet, artichoke-flavored Cynar and citrus bitters stand in for the Aperol in this light, dry cocktail, with rosé vermouth adding a spicy, floral accent. Marianella created the drink on the terrazza (balcony) of a friend's California beach house around sunset.

Ice

3 ounces chilled Prosecco

2 ounces rosé vermouth, preferably Martini Rosato

¾ ounce Cynar

2 dashes of citrus bitters

1 thin orange wedge, preferably blood orange, for garnish

Fill a chilled wineglass with ice. Add all of the remaining ingredients except the garnish and stir well. Garnish the drink with the orange wedge.

"Format" white wine glasses by Rosenthal.

A

the reinvention
JALISCO FLOWER

A huge fan of both tequila and aperitif cocktails, Marianella set out to combine them. "I wanted people to understand that tequila is not just for shots but can be part of a delicious drink before dinner." The result of his efforts is this bright, pleasantly bitter creation.

Ice

¾ ounce St-Germain elderflower liqueur

½ ounce reposado tequila

1 ounce fresh Ruby Red grapefruit juice

4 ounces chilled Prosecco

Fill a cocktail shaker with ice. Add the St-Germain, tequila and grapefruit juice and shake well. Strain into a chilled flute and stir in the Prosecco.

the mocktail
GENTIANA

The Gentiana's mix of citrus juices and tonic water makes it taste like lemonade for grown-ups.

Ice

3 ounces chilled tonic water

1 ounce fresh grapefruit juice

1 ounce fresh orange juice

½ ounce fresh lemon juice

¾ ounce elderflower syrup

1 orange wedge and 1 mint sprig, for garnish

Fill a chilled wineglass with ice. Add the tonic water, citrus juices and elderflower syrup and stir well. Garnish with the orange wedge and mint sprig.

AVIATION

Charlotte Voisey · William Grant & Sons · San Francisco

the classic
AVIATION

The original, 1916 version of the Aviation included crème de violette, a violet-flavored liqueur that tinted the drink a pale sky blue (hence its name, some say). Not much later, the liqueur became nearly impossible to find in the US, and this version of the drink—without any crème de violette—became the standard. (Ironically, at least three new brands of crème de violette have launched within the last decade.)

◇ **Ice**
◇ **1½ ounces gin**
◇ **½ ounce maraschino liqueur**
◇ **½ ounce fresh lemon juice**
◇ **1 lemon twist, for garnish**

◇ Fill a cocktail shaker with ice. Add the gin, maraschino liqueur and lemon juice and shake well. Strain into a chilled coupe and garnish with the lemon twist.

Left to right: "Pebbles" glass by
Moser; "Essence" glass by Iittala;
"Feast" coupe from Huset Shop;
"Fia" carafe from Scandinavian
Design Center; background from
the Antique Mirror Glass Co.

FLIGHT OF FANCY P.33

AVIATION P.29   AVIATION BLUSH SOUR P.32

the twist

AVIATION BLUSH SOUR

Charlotte Voisey loves sour marasca cherries. "They bring such a complex richness to a cocktail, as well as great color," she says. She uses them three ways in this creamy riff on the Aviation, made with crème de violette: muddled; in liqueur form (real maraschino liqueur, which is clear, is made from marasca cherries); and as a simple garnish.

3 brandied cherries

1½ ounces gin

¼ ounce maraschino liqueur

¼ ounce crème de violette (violet liqueur)

1 ounce fresh lemon juice

¼ ounce Simple Syrup (p. 19)

1 large egg white

Ice

1 lemon twist, for garnish

2 jarred marasca cherries skewered on a pick, for garnish (optional)

In a cocktail shaker, muddle the brandied cherries. Add the gin, maraschino liqueur, crème de violette, lemon juice, Simple Syrup and egg white and shake well. Add ice and shake again. Fine-strain (P.18) into a chilled coupe and garnish the drink with the lemon twist and skewered marasca cherries.

the reinvention

FLIGHT OF FANCY

When Voisey makes the mint soda for Flight of Fancy, she uses it right away, to impart a grassy freshness to the drink. (Letting the herbs steep too long makes the soda overly minty.) For the gin she prefers Hendrick's, because unlike classic London dry gins, which have strong spice flavors, it tastes of fresh cucumbers and rose petals.

◇ Ice
◇ 1½ ounces gin
◇ ½ ounce maraschino liqueur
◇ ¾ ounce fresh lemon juice
◇ ½ ounce chilled pineapple juice
◇ ½ ounce orgeat (almond-flavored syrup)
◇ Dash of Peychaud's bitters
◇ 2 ounces Mint Soda (below)
◇ 1 mint sprig plus 1 jarred marasca cherry skewered on a pick with 1 lemon wheel, for garnish
◇ 1 pineapple leaf, for garnish (optional)

Fill a cocktail shaker with ice. Add all of the remaining ingredients except the Mint Soda and garnishes and shake well. Fine-strain (**P.18**) into a chilled, ice-filled collins glass, then stir in the Mint Soda. Garnish the drink with the mint sprig, skewered cherry and lemon wheel and the pineapple leaf.

MINT SODA

Fill a soda siphon (see Note) with 4 ounces cold water and 8 mint leaves. Seal the canister, shake hard and charge twice according to the manufacturer's directions, using 1 or 2 CO_2 chargers; shake well between charges. Use right away. Makes about 4 ounces.
NOTE Soda siphons and CO_2 chargers can be purchased at kitchenware shops and *surlatable.com.*

BEE'S KNEES

Lynnette Marrero · Drinks at 6 · New York City

the classic
BEE'S KNEES

This honey-sweetened Prohibition-era cocktail makes Lynnette Marrero think of spring: "It's simple, clean and refreshing—like a winter toddy that's gotten a spring make-over," she says.

◇ Ice
◇ 2 ounces gin
◇ ¾ ounce fresh lemon juice
◇ ¾ ounce honey syrup (1 tablespoon honey mixed with ½ tablespoon warm water)

◇ Fill a cocktail shaker with ice. Add the gin, lemon juice and honey syrup; shake well. Strain into a chilled coupe.

the twist
DUTCH CLOVER

Inspired by one of her favorite Bee's Knees variations—the Gold Rush, made with bourbon instead of gin—Marrero decided to come up with her own version using Dutch genever, which has a malty, whiskey-like quality. She adds aquavit, too, because its caraway flavor goes so well with the genever.

◇ Ice
◇ 1½ ounces genever, preferably Bols
◇ ½ ounce aquavit
◇ ¾ ounce fresh lemon juice
◇ ¾ ounce honey syrup (1 tablepoon honey mixed with ½ tablepoon warm water)
◇ 1 lemon twist, for garnish

◇ Fill a cocktail shaker with ice. Add the genever, aquavit, lemon juice and honey syrup and shake well. Strain into a chilled coupe and garnish with the lemon twist.

BEE'S KNEES

Champagne coupe from Leo Design.

Marrero thinks this fizzy herbal cocktail would be a great aperitif before a dinner of spring lamb.

the reinvention
LAVENDER-SAGE SLING

Ice

2 ounces gin, preferably Plymouth

1 ounce Lavender-Sage Vermouth (below)

¾ ounce fresh lemon juice

½ ounce honey

2 ounces chilled club soda

1 sage sprig, for garnish

Fill a cocktail shaker with ice. Add the gin, Lavender-Sage Vermouth, lemon juice and honey and shake well. Strain into a chilled, ice-filled collins glass. Stir in the club soda and garnish with the sage sprig.

LAVENDER-SAGE VERMOUTH

In a small saucepan, bring 12 ounces bianco vermouth and 1 tablespoon dried lavender buds to a boil. Cook at a low simmer until reduced by one-third, about 30 minutes. Remove from the heat, add 4 sage sprigs and let stand for 2 hours. Strain the infused vermouth into a jar; refrigerate for up to 3 weeks. Makes about 8 ounces.

the mocktail
BEE'S EASE

Marrero loves mint tea. Infused with lavender, it's the base for this mocktail, which she sweetens with a pale, floral acacia honey syrup. If you're making the drink with a darker, more robust honey such as clover, use ¾ tablespoon each of honey and water.

Ice

2 ounces Lavender-Mint Tea (below)

1 ounce fresh lemon juice

¾ ounce honey syrup (1 tablespoon honey mixed with ½ tablespoon warm water)

1 ounce chilled club soda

1 mint sprig, for garnish

Fill a cocktail shaker with ice. Add the Lavender-Mint Tea, lemon juice and honey syrup and shake well. Strain into a chilled rocks glass, stir in the club soda and garnish with the mint sprig.

LAVENDER-MINT TEA

In a small saucepan, bring 12 ounces water to a low simmer. Remove from the heat, add 1 tablespoon dried lavender buds and 3 mint sprigs and let steep for 5 minutes. Strain the tea into a jar and let cool. The tea can be refrigerated overnight. Makes about 11 ounces.

BELLINI

Dushan Zaric · Employees Only · New York City

 the classic
BELLINI

*Giuseppe Cipriani first
served this cocktail in
1945 to use up an excess
supply of fresh white
peaches at his Harry's Bar
in Venice. Three years
later, Cipriani named the
drink for the Renaissance
painter Giovanni Bellini
during an exhibition of
the artist's work.*

◇ **4½ ounces chilled Prosecco**
◇ **1 ounce white peach puree (see Note)**
◇ **½ ounce crème de framboise (raspberry liqueur)**

◇ In a pint glass, slowly stir the Prosecco into the peach puree. Drizzle in the crème de framboise, then pour the drink into a chilled flute.

NOTE Les Vergers Boiron and the Perfect Purée of Napa Valley (*perfectpuree.com*) both make high-quality fruit purees, including white peach. They're available online and at specialty food stores.

BLOOD PEACH BELLINI P.40

BELLINI

Left to right: "Arcade" flute by Baccarat; "Iskender" flute by Hermès; "Gold Leaf" wallpaper from Donghia.

the twist
GINGER BELLINI

In the mid-1940s, the Bellini was available only when peaches were in season; nowadays, mixologists make the drink year-round using high-quality prepared peach puree. For an autumnal version of this brunch-menu mainstay, Dushan Zaric replaces the original's raspberry liqueur with a ginger-infused peach cordial.

4 ounces chilled Prosecco
1 ounce white peach puree (see Note, p. 38)
¾ ounce Ginger-Peach Liqueur (below)

In a pint glass, slowly stir the Prosecco into the peach puree. Drizzle in the Ginger-Peach Liqueur, then pour into a chilled flute.

GINGER-PEACH LIQUEUR
In a small saucepan, combine 8 ounces crème de pêche with a thinly sliced 1-inch piece of fresh ginger. Bring to a boil, then remove from the heat; let cool slightly. Muddle the ginger into the crème de pêche and let cool for 30 minutes. Pour the infused liqueur through a very fine strainer into a jar and store at room temperature for up to 1 month. Makes about 7 ounces.

the reinvention
BLOOD PEACH BELLINI

The Blood Peach Bellini was originally made using super-seasonal summer blood peaches. This variation combines Campari, grenadine and white peach puree to approximate the rare fruit's flavor and color.

4 ounces chilled Prosecco
½ ounce Campari
1 ounce white peach puree (see Note, p. 38)
½ ounce grenadine, preferably EO (see Note) or homemade (p. 19)

In a pint glass, gently stir all of the ingredients. Pour the drink into a chilled flute.

NOTE EO grenadine, made by the team at Employees Only, is available at *employeesonlybrands.com*.

BLOOD & SAND

Lydia Reissmueller · Tender Bar Cocktail Catering · Portland, OR

the classic
BLOOD & SAND

Debuting around the same time as the silent film Blood and Sand, *starring Rudolph Valentino, this 1920s cocktail is smoky and fruity but not overly sweet, thanks to Heering cherry liqueur. Unlike most cherry liqueurs, it's slightly dry and tart.*

◇ Ice
◇ 1 ounce single-malt Scotch
◇ ¾ ounce Carpano Antica Formula or other sweet vermouth
◇ ¾ ounce Heering cherry liqueur
◇ ¾ ounce fresh orange juice

◇ Fill a cocktail shaker with ice. Add all of the remaining ingredients and shake well. Strain into a chilled coupe.

the twist
FALLEN MATADOR

*Continuing with the film theme (*Blood and Sand *tells the story of the rise and fall of a Spanish bull-fighter), "the Fallen Matador is an inverted Blood & Sand," says Lydia Reissmueller. "The cherry element is in the base spirit (kirsch), and the Scotch element is represented by a liqueur (Drambuie)." The resulting cocktail is drier and spicier than the classic.*

◇ Ice
◇ ¾ ounce kirsch
◇ ¾ ounce Carpano Antica Formula or other sweet vermouth
◇ ½ ounce Drambuie (honeyed Scotch-based liqueur)
◇ ¾ ounce fresh orange juice
◇ Dash of Angostura bitters

◇ Fill a cocktail shaker with ice. Add all of the remaining ingredients and shake well. Strain into a chilled coupe.

the reinvention

SANGRE DE TORO

Reissmueller's lusty, smoky Sangre de Toro ("bull's blood" in Spanish) showcases Spain's prized fortified wine, sherry, as well as two Scotches: a smooth blended one and a pungent, peaty bottling from Islay (Reissmueller opts for Laphroaig).

◇ **Ice**
◇ **1 ounce blended Scotch, preferably Famous Grouse**
◇ **1 ounce East India sherry, preferably Lustau Solera**
◇ **½ ounce single-malt Scotch, preferably Islay**
◇ **1 ounce fresh orange juice**
◇ **3 dashes of cherry bitters**

◇ Fill a cocktail shaker with ice. Add all of the remaining ingredients and shake well. Strain into a chilled coupe.

the mocktail

FIGHTER'S REPRIEVE

Barley malt syrup and cherry preserves add depth, sweetness and complexity to this teetotaling Blood & Sand.

◇ **Ice**
◇ **2 ounces fresh orange juice**
◇ **½ teaspoon cherry preserves**
◇ **½ teaspoon barley malt syrup (molasses-like sweetener)**
◇ **2 cracked black peppercorns**

◇ Fill a cocktail shaker with ice. Add all of the remaining ingredients and shake well. Fine-strain (**P.18**) the drink into a chilled coupe.

FIGHTER'S REPRIEVE

*"Plume" flute by Paola C.; "Arles"
Champagne cup by Ichendorf from
Unica Home.*

BLOODY MARY

Craig Schoettler • The Aviary • Chicago

the classic
BLOODY MARY

"The Bloody Mary is essentially a tomato soup seasoned with alcohol," says Craig Schoettler, who works closely with chef Grant Achatz at his bar Aviary in Chicago. Just as in cooking, Schoettler says, *"the balance of salt is critical."*

◇ Ice
◇ 1½ ounces vodka
◇ 8 ounces chilled tomato juice
◇ ¼ ounce fresh lemon juice
◇ ½ teaspoon Worcestershire sauce, plus more to taste
◇ ½ teaspoon Tabasco, plus more to taste
◇ Salt and freshly ground pepper
◇ 1 celery rib and 1 lemon wedge, for garnish

◇ Fill a chilled collins glass with ice. Add the vodka, tomato juice, lemon juice, Worcestershire sauce and Tabasco and stir well. Season the drink with salt and pepper and garnish with the celery rib and lemon wedge.

the twist
BLOODY MARGARET

For this drink, Schoettler took a tequila-based Bloody Mary (called a Bloody Maria) and added gin. He prefers using Small's, a small-batch gin from Oregon, because it's so botanical: "It has flavors of caraway, cardamom and celery seed, so it pairs well with tomato," he says. (Small's gin is available at ransomspirits.com.)

Ice

1 ounce blanco tequila

½ ounce gin

8 ounces chilled tomato juice

¼ ounce fresh lemon juice

½ teaspoon Worcestershire sauce, plus more to taste

½ teaspoon Tabasco, plus more to taste

Salt and freshly ground pepper

1 celery rib and 1 lemon wedge, for garnish

Fill a chilled collins glass with ice. Add the tequila, gin, tomato juice, lemon juice, Worcestershire sauce and Tabasco and stir well. Season the drink with salt and pepper and garnish with the celery rib and lemon wedge.

the reinvention

AVIARY'S BLOODY MARY

MAKES 2 DRINKS

This deconstructed Bloody Mary can be made year-round with bottled tomato juice, but Schoettler prefers using fresh, ripe tomatoes in the summer. As the colorful ice cubes melt in the cocktail, they slowly season the drink: The green cubes are made with celery, the black ones use Worcestershire sauce and the red cubes get their color and flavor from Fresno chiles. This way, he says, "the palate doesn't get bored. The drink is 'new' with every sip."

◇ **Celery, Fresno Chile and Worcestershire Ice Cubes (below)**
◇ **5½ ounces vodka**
◇ **12 ounces chilled tomato juice**
◇ **¾ ounce Simple Syrup (p. 19)**
◇ **½ teaspoon salt**
◇ **Freshly cracked black pepper, celery ribs and parsley sprigs, for garnish (optional)**

◇ Fill 2 chilled collins glasses with 2 cubes each of the Celery, Fresno Chile and Worcestershire Ice Cubes. In a small pitcher, combine the vodka, tomato juice, Simple Syrup and salt and stir well. Pour the Bloody Mary mixture over the ice cubes and garnish the drinks with cracked black pepper, celery ribs and parsley.

CELERY ICE CUBES
◇ Using a juice extractor, juice 2 blanched celery ribs. Add ½ teaspoon each of salt and sugar to the juice and stir well. Makes 4 cubes in a standard ice tray.

FRESNO CHILE ICE CUBES
◇ Using a juice extractor, juice 2 stemmed Fresno or 6 Thai chiles. Add 4 ounces water to the juice and stir well. Makes 4 cubes in a standard ice tray.

WORCESTERSHIRE ICE CUBES
◇ Combine 2 ounces Worcestershire sauce with 3 ounces water. Makes 4 cubes in a standard ice tray.

AVIARY'S BLOODY MARY

BRANDY CRUSTA

Chris Hannah • Arnaud's French 75 Bar • New Orleans

The Brandy Crusta was invented by Joseph Santini at the City Exchange bar and café in New Orleans around 1850. One of the drink's distinguishing characteristics is its long lemon-peel garnish; it's easily created using a vegetable peeler. (Crusta refers to moistening the rim of a glass, coating it with sugar and letting it dry into a crust.)

the classic
BRANDY CRUSTA

- 1 lemon wedge and sugar
- 1 long strip of lemon zest, for garnish
- Ice
- 1½ ounces VSOP Cognac
- ½ ounce orange curaçao
- ¼ ounce maraschino liqueur
- ½ ounce fresh lemon juice
- 2 dashes of Angostura bitters

Moisten a rocks glass rim with the wedge; coat with sugar. Add the zest to the glass. Fill a shaker with ice. Add the remaining ingredients; shake well. Strain into the glass.

At Arnaud's French 75 Bar (just four blocks from the bar where Santini worked), Chris Hannah makes this apple-accented riff on the Brandy Crusta using Calvados instead of the classic's Cognac.

the twist
POMME EN CROUTE

- 1 orange wedge and sugar
- 1 long strip of orange zest, for garnish
- Ice
- 1½ ounces Calvados
- ½ ounce orange curaçao
- ½ ounce Gran Classico amaro or Campari
- ½ ounce fresh lemon juice

Moisten half of a rocks glass rim with the wedge; coat with sugar. Add the zest. Fill a shaker with ice. Add the remaining ingredients; shake well. Strain into the glass.

POMME EN CROUTE

B

the reinvention

CHERRY BLOSSOM BROCADE

While Hannah loves making classic cocktails, he also enjoys tinkering with them to come up with new drinks. The licoricey Cherry Blossom Brocade uses three ingredients that weren't available in the US when the Brandy Crusta was invented a century and a half ago: whiskey-like Dutch genever, Heering cherry liqueur and absinthe.

1 lemon wedge and sugar

1 long strip of grapefruit zest, for garnish

Ice

1½ ounces genever, preferably Bols

½ ounce Heering cherry liqueur

¼ ounce absinthe

¾ ounce fresh Ruby Red grapefruit juice

2 dashes of grapefruit bitters

Moisten half of the outer rim of a chilled rocks glass with the lemon wedge and coat lightly with sugar. Arrange the grapefruit zest in the glass. Fill a cocktail shaker with ice. Add the genever, cherry liqueur, absinthe, grapefruit juice and bitters to the shaker and shake well. Strain the drink into the prepared rocks glass.

BRONX

Derek Brown · Columbia Room · Washington, DC

the classic
BRONX

The Bronx became a popular drink around 1910, possibly because it was one of the first to contain orange juice. Serious cocktail drinkers considered the Bronx weak, but Derek Brown calls it "a perfectly balanced hot-weather cocktail."

Ice
1½ ounces London dry gin
½ ounce sweet vermouth
½ ounce dry vermouth
1 ounce fresh orange juice

Fill a cocktail shaker with ice. Add all of the remaining ingredients and shake well. Strain into a chilled coupe.

the twist
INCOME TAX COCKTAIL

"The seasoned bartender knows that when you create a drink you're really just borrowing from another cocktail recipe," says Brown. "The fact is, we create very little, adding an ingredient here or deleting one there. The Income Tax Cocktail is virtually identical to the Bronx in all ways but one: the addition of aromatic bitters. But what a difference it makes."

Ice
1½ ounces London dry gin
½ ounce sweet vermouth
½ ounce dry vermouth
1 ounce fresh orange juice
Dash of Fee Brothers Old Fashion aromatic bitters

Fill a cocktail shaker with ice. Add all of the remaining ingredients and shake well. Strain into a chilled coupe.

the reinvention
THE TAX LAWYER

For this potent riff on the Bronx—Brown calls it "a Bronx with teeth"—he cut down the orange juice, replaced the gin with rich, malty genever and added a dash of the bitter Italian digestif Fernet-Branca.

Ice

1½ ounces genever, preferably Bols

¾ ounce sweet vermouth

¾ ounce dry vermouth

½ teaspoon Fernet-Branca

½ teaspoon fresh orange juice

1 orange twist, for garnish

Fill a pint glass with ice. Add all of the remaining ingredients except the garnish and stir well. Strain into a chilled coupe and garnish with the orange twist.

the mocktail
TAX-FREE DAY

Chinotto is a citrusy, cola-colored Italian soda made from a small sour orange of the same name. Brown likes using the soda in mocktails because it's both bitter and sweet. The aromatic bitters in the drink are alcohol-based; they can be left out of the drink.

Ice

1½ ounces chilled chinotto (see Note)

1½ ounces fresh orange juice

2 dashes of Fee Brothers Old Fashion aromatic bitters (optional)

1 or 2 mint sprigs and 1 orange twist, for garnish

Fill a chilled highball glass with ice. Add the chinotto, orange juice and bitters and stir gently. Garnish the drink with the mint sprigs and orange twist.

NOTE San Pellegrino chinotto is available at Italian and specialty markets and *ditalia.com.*

TAX-FREE DAY

"Pleats" highball by Donna
Karan Lenox.

TROPICAL COCKTAIL BASICS

Almost all tropical drinks have three ingredients in common: citrus (juice or muddled pieces), sugar (in granular or syrup form) and a sugar-based spirit. The Caipirinha includes muddled limes, raw sugar and sugarcane-based Brazilian cachaça. Substitute molasses-based rum for the cachaça, squeeze the limes instead of muddling them and use simple syrup and you have a Daiquiri, Cuba's famous drink. Go with rum again but add mint and club soda and it's Mojito time. Add an exotic liqueur or two and you're foraying into tiki territory. Just don't forget the paper umbrella.

CAIPIRINHA

John Lermayer · Blackbird Ordinary · Miami

the classic
CAIPIRINHA

Caipirinha, Brazil's national cocktail, roughly translates as "little countryside drink." Its foundation is sugarcane-based cachaça, long considered a coarse peasant product. Now, excellent artisanal cachaças are widely available in the US.

- 1 small lime, cut into 6 wedges
- 1 tablespoon Demerara or other raw sugar
- Crushed ice
- 2 ounces cachaça

In a chilled double rocks glass, muddle the lime wedges and sugar. Fill the glass halfway with crushed ice and stir well. Stir in the cachaça, then stir in more crushed ice.

the twist
GRAND MARNIER SMASH

John Lermayer describes the Grand Marnier Smash as having "the same script" as the Caipirinha but different characters: lemon instead of lime and Grand Marnier instead of cachaça and sugar, plus lots of muddled mint.

- ½ lemon, cut into 6 wedges
- 10 mint leaves, plus 1 mint sprig for garnish
- Crushed ice
- 2 ounces Grand Marnier

In a chilled double rocks glass, muddle the lemon wedges and mint leaves. Add crushed ice and the Grand Marnier and stir well. Garnish with the mint sprig.

the reinvention
SANDIA SMASH

"No single ingredient is more appealing than fresh watermelon," says Lermayer. "The second I serve one of these Caipirinhas, everyone else wants the same."

3 watermelon chunks, plus 3 watermelon chunks skewered on a pick for garnish

Ice

¾ ounce fresh lime juice

¼ ounce agave nectar

½ ounce St-Germain elderflower liqueur

2 ounces blanco tequila

In a cocktail shaker, muddle the 3 watermelon chunks. Add ice and the lime juice, agave nectar, St-Germain and blanco tequila and shake well. Fine-strain (**P.18**) into a chilled, ice-filled collins glass and garnish the drink with the skewered watermelon chunks.

SANDIA SMASH

Tumbler by Karl Lagerfeld for Orrefors; "High Society" glass by NasonMoretti from TableArt.

CHAMPAGNE COCKTAIL

Jamie Boudreau • Canon: Whiskey & Bitters Emporium • Seattle

the classic
CHAMPAGNE COCKTAIL

According to master mixologist Dale DeGroff, this is one of the few original cocktails that appeared in the first (1862) version of the seminal How to Mix Drinks *by Jerry Thomas. The recipe has remained unchanged for 150 years.*

1 **sugar cube**

3 **dashes of Angostura bitters**

5 **ounces chilled brut Champagne**

1 **lemon twist, for garnish**

In a small dish or glass, soak the sugar cube with the Angostura bitters. Fill a chilled flute with the Champagne, then add the bitters-soaked sugar cube. Garnish the drink with the lemon twist.

CHAMPAGNE COCKTAIL

"Vitis" Champagne glass by Riedel; "Murano" cut-glass bowl from The End of History.

the twist
SPARKLING MONK

Green Chartreuse, a spicy French liqueur tinted by the 100-plus plants that flavor it, gives this cocktail a lovely pale lime color.

1 sugar cube

¼ ounce green Chartreuse

½ ounce Licor 43 (citrus-and-vanilla-flavored Spanish liqueur)

4 ounces chilled brut Champagne

1 lime twist, for garnish

In a small dish or glass, soak the sugar cube with the Chartreuse. Pour the Licor 43 into a chilled flute, then add the Champagne. Drop in the Chartreuse-soaked sugar cube and garnish with the lime twist.

the reinvention
ARANCIONE COCKTAIL

To transform the Champagne Cocktail into a sweet and intense after-dinner drink, Jamie Boudreau swaps out the sparkling wine for Cocchi Americano, a bittersweet aperitif wine. The ounce of club soda makes the cocktail lightly bubbly; Boudreau likes to make the drink in a soda siphon for extra fizz.

4 ounces Cocchi Americano

¼ ounce each of Amaro Montenegro and Ramazzotti (bittersweet herbal liqueurs)

Dash of orange bitters

Dash of Angostura bitters

Ice

1 ounce chilled club soda

Fill a soda siphon (see Note) with all of the ingredients except ice and the club soda. Seal the canister and shake hard. Charge according to the manufacturer's directions, using a CO_2 charger. Dispense into a chilled, ice-filled wineglass and top with the club soda.

NOTE Soda siphons and CO_2 chargers can be purchased at kitchenware shops and *surlatable.com*.

CORPSE REVIVER NO. 2

John deBary · PDT · New York City

the classic
CORPSE REVIVER NO. 2

"I have an affinity for equal-part cocktails," says John deBary. "Something about the symmetry of the proportions appeals to me." There are a number of Corpse Reviver variations, but this one, from Harry Craddock's 1930 Savoy Cocktail Book, is considered the classic.

¼ ounce absinthe

Ice

¾ ounce London dry gin

¾ ounce Lillet blanc

¾ ounce triple sec

¾ ounce fresh lemon juice

Rinse a chilled coupe with the absinthe and pour out the excess. Fill a cocktail shaker with ice. Add the gin, Lillet blanc, triple sec and lemon juice and shake well. Strain into the prepared glass.

the twist

DEATH AT THE SAVOY

"Adding a splash of sparkling wine is one of the most reliable of cocktail augmentations," says deBary. "Here it creates something of a love child between the classic Corpse Reviver No. 2 and a Death in the Afternoon" (absinthe and Champagne with a lemon twist).

¼ ounce absinthe

Ice

¾ ounce London dry gin

¾ ounce triple sec

½ ounce fresh lemon juice

1 ounce chilled sparkling wine

1 lemon twist, for garnish

Rinse a chilled coupe with the absinthe and pour out the excess. Fill a cocktail shaker with ice. Add the gin, triple sec and lemon juice and shake well. Strain into the prepared glass, top with the wine and garnish with the twist.

the reinvention

JAPANOPHILE

"It's no secret that I'm a Japanophile," says deBary. He has studied the language since middle school and briefly lived in Kyoto. Many of the main ingredients in this drink come from East Asia: sake, shochu (a clear distilled spirit) and a little sour yuzu juice, from the Japanese citrus fruit.

Ice

¾ ounce aquavit

¾ ounce barley *shochu*

¾ ounce *daiginjo* or *ginjo* sake

½ ounce fresh orange juice

½ ounce yuzu juice

½ teaspoon cane syrup (see Note) or Simple Syrup (p. 19)

Fill a cocktail shaker with ice. Add all of the remaining ingredients and shake well. Strain into a chilled coupe.
NOTE Sweet, thick cane syrup is available at Whole Foods and *cocktailkingdom.com*.

JAPANOPHILE

"Serenade" coupe by Theresienthal from TableArt.

SHOW-OFF COCKTAILS

The popularity of the fuchsia-hued Cosmo speaks to a reason many people love cocktails: We drink them to be noticed. Some of the most popular drinks in the world are the most garish: the bright red Singapore Sling (**p.153**) with its cherry-and-pineapple-wedge garnish, the Bloody Mary (**p.44**) with its enormous celery stalk, the Piña Colada with its paper umbrella. Back in the 1990s, the Cosmopolitan became the drink of choice for the trend-obsessed. (Its base spirit, citrus vodka, was actually one of the trendiest of its time.) And Cosmo drinkers were definitely noticed at the bar.

COSMOPOLITAN

Patricia Richards • Wynn Las Vegas • Las Vegas

the classic
COSMOPOLITAN

The Cosmo was invented in the 1980s when Miami Beach bartender Cheryl Cook was developing cocktails for the new Absolut Citron. Starting with a recipe for the Harpoon (vodka, cranberry and lime juice), from a 1960s Ocean Spray ad, Cook added orange liqueur and citrus vodka. Patricia Richards mixes in simple syrup to offset the tartness.

◇ **Ice**
◇ **1½ ounces citrus vodka**
◇ **½ ounce Cointreau or other triple sec**
◇ **¾ ounce chilled cranberry juice**
◇ **½ ounce fresh lime juice**
◇ **½ teaspoon Simple Syrup (p. 19)**
◇ **1 lemon twist, for garnish**

◇ Fill a cocktail shaker with ice. Add the vodka, Cointreau, juices and Simple Syrup and shake well. Strain into a chilled martini glass and garnish with the lemon twist.

the twist
WHITE COSMOPOLITAN

Richards's White Cosmo might be a good choice for anyone embarrassed to be seen drinking Sex and the City's signature cocktail, with its telltale pink color. She created the drink a few years ago; right away it started outselling the classic version, and it's still more popular.

◇ **Ice**
◇ **2 ounces vodka, preferably Level**
◇ **½ ounce Cointreau or other triple sec**
◇ **1 ounce chilled white cranberry juice**
◇ **½ ounce fresh lime juice**
◇ **½ teaspoon Simple Syrup (p. 19)**
◇ **3 frozen cranberries, for garnish**

◇ Fill a cocktail shaker with ice. Add the vodka, Cointreau, juices and Simple Syrup and shake well. Strain into a chilled martini glass and garnish with the cranberries.

C

the reinvention
BLUEBERRY COSMOPOLITAN

For anyone who wants to flaunt a love of Cosmos, muddled blueberries tint this version a gorgeous hot pink. Richards developed the recipe for a spring-summer menu at Wynn Las Vegas's Parasol Down bar at the height of blueberry season.

◇ 8 **blueberries, plus 3 blueberries skewered on a pick for garnish**

◇ **Ice**

◇ 2 **ounces vodka**

◇ ½ **ounce St-Germain elderflower liqueur**

◇ ½ **ounce chilled white cranberry juice**

◇ ½ **ounce fresh lemon juice**

◇ ½ **ounce Simple Syrup (p. 19)**

◇ In a cocktail shaker, muddle the 8 blueberries. Add ice and all of the remaining ingredients except the garnish and shake well. Fine-strain (**P.18**) into a chilled martini glass and garnish with the skewered blueberries.

BLUEBERRY COSMOPOLITAN

"Mod" martini glass by Artel from Tabula Tua; tumbler by Karl Lagerfeld for Orrefors; "Series B" shot glass from Neue Galerie.

DAIQUIRI

Leo Robitschek · Eleven Madison Park · New York City

D

the classic
DAIQUIRI

Daiquiris often mean frozen drinks flavored with commercial sour mix and cheap rum. Leo Robitschek loves introducing people to the real deal: "They're shocked that three simple ingredients can create such a complex drink."

Ice

2 ounces white rum
¾ ounce fresh lime juice
¾ ounce Simple Syrup (p. 19)

Fill a cocktail shaker with ice. Add the rum, lime juice and Simple Syrup and shake well. Strain into a chilled coupe.

the twist
IRON MINE

Cane syrup is richer and sweeter than simple syrup, giving this Daiquiri variation a more sophisticated flavor and velvety texture. Robitschek balances the sweetness by increasing the amount of lime juice and adding a dash of Angostura bitters.

Ice

2 ounces white rum
1 ounce fresh lime juice
½ ounce cane syrup (see Note)
Dash of Angostura bitters

Fill a cocktail shaker with ice. Add the rum, lime juice and cane syrup and shake well. Strain into a chilled coupe and top with the bitters.

NOTE Sweet, thick cane syrup is available at Whole Foods and *cocktailkingdom.com*.

DAIQUIRI

"Eleanor" coupe from William Yeoward Crystal; cocktail shaker from Leo Design.

the reinvention

HEART OF STONE DAIQUIRI

The subtle apricot flavor of this nutty winter Daiquiri and the allspice dram used to rinse the glass remind Robitschek of holiday fruitcake.

¼ ounce St. Elizabeth allspice dram (rum-based allspice liqueur)

Ice

1 ounce white rum

¾ ounce amontillado sherry

½ ounce apricot liqueur

½ ounce fresh lemon juice

¼ ounce cane syrup (see Note)

Rinse a chilled coupe with the allspice dram and pour out the excess. Fill a cocktail shaker with ice. Add all of the remaining ingredients and shake well. Strain the drink into the prepared glass.

NOTE Sweet, thick cane syrup is available at Whole Foods and *cocktailkingdom.com*.

EL DIABLO

Sean Kenyon • Williams & Graham • Denver

the classic
EL DIABLO

As with so many classic cocktails, El Diablo's provenance is hard to pin down. Some say it was created in the 1940s by an unidentified bartender in California. One verifiable fact: It appeared in the 1947 Trader Vic's Bartender's Guide as the Mexican El Diablo and was one of the first tequila drinks.

Ice
1½ ounces blanco tequila
½ ounce crème de cassis (black-currant liqueur)
3 ounces chilled ginger beer
½ ounce fresh lime juice
1 lime wheel, for garnish

Fill a chilled collins glass with ice. Add all of the remaining ingredients except the garnish and stir well. Garnish the drink with the lime wheel.

the twist
LA VIDA DEL DIABLO

The combination of ginger beer and Angostura in this mezcal-based Diablo evokes Chinese five-spice powder. Sean Kenyon prefers making the drink with Del Maguey's Mezcal Vida (the company's newest and most affordable mezcal) because it adds great punch and depth.

Ice
1½ ounces mezcal
½ ounce crème de cassis (black-currant liqueur)
3 ounces chilled ginger beer
½ ounce fresh lime juice
2 dashes of Angostura bitters

Fill a chilled collins glass with ice. Add the mezcal, crème de cassis, ginger beer, lime juice and bitters; stir well.

the reinvention

EL DIABLO REFINADO

A short drink is composed mainly of spirits and served without ice. A long drink is served in a tall glass with soda, beer or sparkling wine. Kenyon likes making short drinks long and long ones short. He calls it the "Willy Wonka effect." Here, he shrinks the El Diablo by using ginger liqueur in place of the beer and lemon bitters for the lime juice.

¼ ounce mezcal

Ice

2 ounces blanco tequila

½ ounce crème de mûre (blackberry liqueur)

½ ounce ginger liqueur

2 dashes of lemon bitters

1 lemon twist, for garnish

Rinse a chilled coupe with the mezcal and pour out the excess. Fill a pint glass with ice. Add all of the remaining ingredients except the garnish and stir well. Strain into the prepared coupe and garnish with the lemon twist.

the mocktail

EL DIABLO SOBRIO

Blackberries tint this "Sober Devil" fuchsia. Pink peppercorns together with oil from the lime skins mimic spicy tequila.

6 pink peppercorns

½ lime, cut into quarters

5 blackberries

6 ounces chilled ginger beer

Ice

1 lime wheel, for garnish

In a pint glass, muddle the peppercorns, lime quarters and 4 blackberries with 2 ounces of the ginger beer. Fine-strain (**P.18**) into an ice-filled collins glass, then stir in the remaining ginger beer. Garnish with the remaining blackberry and the lime wheel.

EL DIABLO REFINADO

"Series B" coupes from Neue Galerie;
"Elijah" antiqued mirror by Oly Studio.

FRENCH 75

Kathy Casey · Kathy Casey Liquid Kitchen · Seattle

CITRUS 75 P.77

Left to right: "Bubble" cocktail glass by Dorothy Thorpe from Replacements, Ltd.; "Vertigo" cocktail pick by Christofle; "Simple" flute by Nouvel Studio; "Patrician" Champagne cup by Lobmeyr from Neue Galerie.

FRENCH 75 P.76

LUXURY PEACH 75 P.76

the classic
FRENCH 75

Many believe this drink was devised by American soldiers in World War I hankering for a Tom Collins. They had gin and lemons but no soda, so they used what was at hand: Champagne. The result was named for the French-made 75-millimeter guns used in the war.

Ice
- 1   ounce gin
- ½   ounce fresh lemon juice
- ½   ounce Simple Syrup (p. 19)
- 4   ounces chilled brut Champagne

Fill a cocktail shaker with ice. Add the gin, lemon juice and Simple Syrup and shake well. Strain into a chilled flute and stir in the Champagne.

the twist
LUXURY PEACH 75

Peach puree and fresh tarragon flavor this summery riff on the French 75. The cocktail is terrific with fresh thyme, too.

- 2   tarragon sprigs
- Ice
- 1   ounce gin
- ½   ounce Cognac
- ¾   ounce fresh lemon juice
- 2   tablespoons peach puree (see Note)
- ½   ounce Simple Syrup (p. 19)
- ½   ounce chilled brut Champagne

Tear 1 tarragon sprig and drop it into a cocktail shaker. Add ice and the gin, Cognac, lemon juice, peach puree and Simple Syrup and shake well. Fine-strain (P.18) into a chilled coupe. Top with the Champagne and garnish with the remaining tarragon sprig.

NOTE Les Vergers Boiron and the Perfect Purée of Napa Valley (*perfectpuree.com*) both make high-quality fruit purees, including a peach variety. They're available online and at specialty food stores.

the reinvention
CITRUS 75

Kathy Casey likes making her own limoncello, the sweet Italian lemon liqueur, for this drink. (You can watch a video at liquidkitchen.tv.) Pallini limoncello, which is widely available, also works well here.

◇ ½ **clementine**
◇ **Ice**
◇ 1½ **ounces gin**
◇ ½ **ounce limoncello**
◇ ¾ **ounce fresh lemon juice**
◇ ½ **ounce honey syrup (½ tablespoon honey mixed with ½ tablespoon warm water)**
◇ 1 **ounce chilled brut Champagne**
◇ 1 **lemon twist and 1 orange wheel, for garnish**

◇ In a cocktail shaker, muddle the clementine. Add ice and the gin, limoncello, lemon juice and honey syrup and shake well. Strain into a chilled coupe, top with the Champagne and garnish with the lemon twist and orange wheel.

Left to right: Stirrer by Gorham; "Madison Square" highball by Kate Spade New York; "Cluny" highball by Christofle; "Random Cut" highball by Calvin Klein; "Bonny Branch" stirrer from BHLDN.

GIN & TONIC P.80

RUM & TONIC P.80

GIN & TONIC

Todd Thrasher · Restaurant Eve · Alexandria, VA

GIN & "TONIC" P.81

A
B
C
D
E
F

G

H
I
J
K
L
M
N
O
P
Q
R
S
T
U
V
W
X
Y
Z

■ *the classic*
GIN & TONIC

The Gin & Tonic is one of Todd Thrasher's favorite cocktails, but with two conditions: The ice must be large enough to melt slowly and the tonic should be high-quality.

Ice

1½ ounces gin, preferably Plymouth

4 ounces chilled tonic water, preferably Schweppes

1 or 2 lime wedges, for garnish

Fill a chilled highball glass with ice. Add the gin and tonic water and stir well. Garnish with the lime wedge.

■ *the twist*
RUM & TONIC

Thrasher says this cocktail puts him in vacation mode. He's a longtime scuba diver, and when he visits the Caribbean island of Bonaire, this is his go-to drink after a day in the water.

Ice

2 ounces white rum, preferably Banks 5-Island

5 ounces chilled tonic water, preferably Fever-Tree premium Indian tonic water

2 dashes of lemon bitters

1 lemon wheel, for garnish

Fill a chilled highball glass with ice. Add the rum, tonic water and lemon bitters and stir well. Garnish the drink with the lemon wheel.

the reinvention
GIN & "TONIC"

It took about nine months for Thrasher to perfect his recipe for homemade tonic syrup. "I have it down now and it's my absolute favorite," he says. Cinchona bark powder (which contains tonic water's signature quinine) can be purchased from the Dandelion Botanical Company (dandelionbotanical.com).

Ice
2 ounces gin, preferably Citadelle Réserve
1½ ounces Tonic Syrup (below)
2 dashes of lemon bitters
4 ounces chilled club soda
1 lemon twist, for garnish

Fill a highball glass with ice. Add the gin, Tonic Syrup and bitters; stir well. Stir in the soda. Garnish with the twist.

TONIC SYRUP

In a large saucepan, bring 16 ounces water to a boil. Stir in ½ cup sugar until dissolved. Whisk in 1 tablespoon honey, ½ coarsely chopped lemongrass stalk (tender inner core only), ¼ teaspoon dried lavender buds and ½ tablespoon cinchona bark powder (above left). Simmer over low heat until reduced by half, about 45 minutes. Strain through a fine sieve, then a fine coffee filter and finally through a paper coffee filter. Let cool, then add ½ ounce each of lemon juice and lime juice. Refrigerate the syrup for up to 2 weeks. Makes about 10 ounces.

the mocktail
MOCKTAIL FOR T.

Thrasher created this drink in honor of his one-year-old son, Trystan. The recipe calls for lemon bitters, a concentrated, alcohol-based, lemon-infused tincture; omit them to make the drink totally alcohol-free.

Ice
5 ounces chilled club soda
2 ounces Tonic Syrup (above)
2 dashes of lemon bitters (optional)
1 lemon twist, for garnish

Fill a highball glass with ice. Add the club soda, Tonic Syrup and bitters; stir well. Garnish with the lemon twist.

HOT COCKTAILS 101

Mixologists are clearly obsessed with temperature when it comes to chilled cocktails: They hand-cut ice cubes and keep different spirits at different temperatures. Some even check finished cocktails with a thermometer. Hot drinks require similar attention to detail. For toddies, mulled wine and Irish Coffee–style drinks, mixing at a not-too-hot temperature is key. Experts make sure that the coffee, tea or water isn't warmer than 173°F. (That's the temperature at which many spirits boil; as the alcohol evaporates, the drink's aroma can become over-powering.) One benefit of Irish Coffee's whipped cream topping: It acts as a lid, keeping the alcohol's vapors from escaping.

IRISH COFFEE

Bryan Dayton • Oak at Fourteenth • Boulder, CO

the classic
IRISH COFFEE

San Francisco's Buena Vista restaurant claims to have made America's first Irish Coffee, in 1952. One of their patrons, a travel writer named Stanton Delaplane, tasted the drink at Shannon Airport in Ireland and helped the restaurant re-create it.

2 teaspoons light brown sugar

3 ounces hot brewed coffee

1½ ounces Irish whiskey, preferably Bushmills

Dollop of unsweetened whipped cream, for garnish

In a warmed mug or heatproof glass, stir the sugar into the coffee until dissolved. Stir in the whiskey, then garnish the drink with the whipped cream.

the twist
MAYAN COFFEE

For his Mexican riff on Irish Coffee, Bryan Dayton swaps in tequila for the whiskey, sweetens the drink with agave nectar and dusts the top with ground cinnamon.

2 teaspoons agave nectar

3 ounces hot brewed coffee

1½ ounces tequila, preferably El Tesoro añejo

Dollop of unsweetened whipped cream and pinch of ground cinnamon, for garnish

In a warmed mug or heatproof glass, stir the agave nectar into the coffee until incorporated. Stir in the tequila, then garnish with the whipped cream and cinnamon.

the reinvention

THE WITCHES' COFFEE

MAKES 4 DRINKS

To underscore the rich flavor of dark Sumatra coffee, Dayton mixes it with aged rum, spicy, saffron-based Strega and molasses-y raw sugar. He even spices up the whipped cream, with bittersweet Italian Averna.

◇   **4** teaspoons Demerara or other raw sugar
◇ **12** ounces hot brewed coffee
◇   **6** ounces aged rum, preferably Ron Zacapa 23
◇   **3** ounces Strega (saffron-infused liqueur)
◇ **Averna Cream (below), for garnish**

◇ In a heatproof pitcher, stir the sugar into the coffee until dissolved, then stir in the rum and Strega. Pour the coffee into warmed mugs or heatproof glasses and spoon the Averna Cream on top.

AVERNA CREAM

◇ In a medium chilled bowl, whip 4 ounces chilled heavy cream with 1 ounce Averna amaro and ½ tablespoon granulated sugar until soft peaks form. Use the cream immediately. Makes enough for 4 drinks.

THE WITCHES' COFFEE

the mocktail

ST. STEVEN'S
WINTER WARMER

MAKES 4 DRINKS

For this mocktail, Dayton flavors coffee with 1883 de Philibert Routin non-alcoholic rum syrup (Torani makes another widely available version). The recipe for Dayton's lavender-scented whipped cream can be doubled and the extra used as a topping for pie or cake. Extra lavender syrup can be stirred into club soda or poured over ice cream.

12 ounces hot coffee
 4 ounces rum syrup or butter rum syrup
Lavender Whipped Cream (below) and a drizzle
   of honey, for garnish

In a heatproof pitcher, combine the coffee and rum syrup. Stir well and pour into warmed mugs or heatproof glasses. Garnish with the Lavender Whipped Cream and honey.

LAVENDER WHIPPED CREAM

In a small saucepan, simmer 1 ounce Simple Syrup (P.19) with ¾ teaspoon dried lavender buds until fragrant, about 5 minutes. Strain and let cool. In a chilled bowl, whip the lavender syrup with 4 ounces chilled heavy cream until soft peaks form. Use right away. Makes enough for 4 drinks.

JACK ROSE

Jackson Cannon • The Hawthorne • Boston

the classic
JACK ROSE

*This Jack Rose is based
on the recipe in Stanley
Clisby Arthur's 1937 book*
Famous New Orleans
Drinks and How to Mix
'Em. *"Arthur is a god
to us up here in Boston,
where we have a deep
appreciation for New
Orleans's contribution
to our cocktail culture,"
says Jackson Cannon.*

Ice

2 ounces Laird's bonded apple brandy

¾ ounce grenadine, preferably homemade (p. 19)

½ ounce fresh lemon juice

Dash of Peychaud's bitters

1 lemon twist, for garnish

Fill a cocktail shaker with ice. Add all of the remaining ingredients except the garnish and shake well. Strain into a chilled coupe and garnish with the lemon twist.

the twist
ROSÉ DE JACQUES

*This is simply a Jack Rose
made with Calvados.
According to Cannon, its
apple flavor is far more
concentrated: "In that
first cold snap of fall when
we've broken out our
sweaters, the lush apple
flavors of this version
seem just right."*

Ice

2 ounces Calvados

¾ ounce grenadine, preferably homemade (p. 19)

½ ounce fresh lemon juice

Dash of Peychaud's bitters

1 lemon twist, for garnish

Fill a cocktail shaker with ice. Add all of the remaining ingredients except the garnish and shake well. Strain into a chilled coupe and garnish with the lemon twist.

the reinvention
STONE ROSE

When Cannon was growing up in Virginia, he would suck the nectar out of the honeysuckle flowers that grew on the long fence across from his house. This sparkling, pear-scented cocktail reminds him of that time. Leftover spiced syrup can be stirred into tea or lemonade or poured over fresh fruit.

Ice

1 ounce pear brandy

¾ ounce rosé vermouth

¾ ounce Spiced Honey Syrup (below)

½ ounce fresh lemon juice

Dash of Peychaud's bitters

1 ounce chilled cava or other dry sparkling wine

Fill a cocktail shaker with ice. Add all of the remaining ingredients except the cava and shake well. Strain into a large chilled coupe and top with the cava.

SPICED HONEY SYRUP

Wrap ½ cinnamon stick and 2 green cardamom pods in a kitchen towel and crush with a mallet or heavy pan. In a small saucepan, combine ½ cup honey with 4 ounces water. Add 1 tablespoon chopped fresh ginger and the crushed spices and simmer over moderate heat, stirring frequently, until the syrup darkens and the spices are very aromatic, about 15 minutes. Let cool, then cover and refrigerate until chilled and infused, at least 8 hours. Pour the syrup through a fine strainer into a clean jar and refrigerate for up to 2 weeks. Makes about 6 ounces.

STONE ROSE

LAST WORD

Joaquín Simó • Death & Co. • New York City

NAKED & FAMOUS

FINAL WARD

"Alto" coupe by Calvin Klein;
martini glass by Deborah Ehrlich
from E.R. Butler & Co.

the classic
LAST WORD

The junipery Last Word is an early Prohibition cocktail. Fairly obscure, it has been popping up on classics-focused menus since venerable Seattle bartender Murray Stenson unearthed its recipe from a 1952 edition of Ted Saucier's Bottoms Up.

- Ice
- ¾ ounce gin
- ¾ ounce green Chartreuse
- ¾ ounce maraschino liqueur
- ¾ ounce fresh lime juice

Fill a cocktail shaker with ice. Add all of the remaining ingredients and shake well. Strain into a chilled coupe.

the twist
FINAL WARD

After getting hooked on the Last Word, Joaquín Simó's friend Phil Ward (of NYC's Mayahuel) tried replacing the gin with Rittenhouse 100-proof rye. "It's a whiskey sour for people who crave complexity," says Simó.

- Ice
- ¾ ounce bonded rye whiskey
- ¾ ounce green Chartreuse
- ¾ ounce maraschino liqueur
- ¾ ounce fresh lemon juice

Fill a cocktail shaker with ice. Add all of the remaining ingredients and shake well. Strain into a chilled coupe.

the reinvention
NAKED & FAMOUS

"Because there is so little mezcal in this cocktail, choosing a big, aggressively smoky bottling is key," says Simó. He opts for Del Maguey's nicely complex Chichicapa.

- Ice
- ¾ ounce mezcal
- ¾ ounce yellow Chartreuse
- ¾ ounce Aperol (bitter orange Italian aperitif)
- ¾ ounce fresh lime juice

Fill a cocktail shaker with ice. Add all of the remaining ingredients and shake well. Strain into a chilled coupe.

MAI TAI

Marco Dionysos · Smuggler's Cove · San Francisco

the classic
MAI TAI

Victor "Trader Vic" Bergeron created the Mai Tai in 1944 using a special supply of 17-year-old imported Jamaican rum. Since this rum is no longer produced, Marco Dionysos uses a blend of aged rums to approximate its flavor.

Crushed ice

- 1 ounce aged dark rum, preferably Jamaican
- 1 ounce aged Martinique rum
- ½ ounce orange curaçao
- ¾ ounce fresh lime juice, lime shell reserved for garnish
- ½ ounce orgeat (almond-flavored syrup)
- 1 mint sprig, for garnish

Fill a cocktail shaker with crushed ice. Add both rums, the curaçao, lime juice and orgeat and shake well. Pour the drink unstrained into a chilled double rocks glass and garnish with the lime shell and mint sprig.

MAI TAI

the twist

BLUEGRASS MAI TAI

Inspired by the use of multiple rums in many tiki drinks, Dionysos concocted a Mai Tai variation calling for two kinds of whiskey: bourbon, which is traditionally from Kentucky bluegrass country, and rye.

Crushed ice

1 ounce bourbon, preferably Maker's Mark

1 ounce bonded rye whiskey, preferably Rittenhouse 100

½ ounce Grand Marnier

1 ounce fresh lemon juice

½ ounce orgeat (almond-flavored syrup)

Powdered sugar and 1 mint sprig, for garnish

Fill a cocktail shaker with crushed ice. Add the bourbon, rye whiskey, Grand Marnier, lemon juice and orgeat and shake well. Pour the drink unstrained into a chilled double rocks glass and add more crushed ice. Sift powdered sugar over the mint sprig and garnish the drink.

the reinvention

■ MAI TAI CHI

"I like the way the chai syrup makes this a more exotic drink while still honoring the classic," says Dionysos. Topping the cocktail with a pinch of cinnamon highlights the spice in the chai. Leftover syrup can be used to pump up the flavor of regular iced tea or stirred into warm milk.

◇ **Crushed ice**
◇ **2 ounces amber rum**
◇ **½ ounce Licor 43**
   (citrus-and-vanilla-flavored Spanish liqueur)
◇ **1 ounce fresh lime juice**
◇ **½ ounce Chai Syrup (below)**
◇ **¼ ounce orgeat (almond-flavored syrup)**
◇ **1 mint sprig, 1 lime wheel and a pinch**
   of ground cinnamon, for garnish

◇ Fill a cocktail shaker with crushed ice. Add the rum, Licor 43, lime juice, Chai Syrup and orgeat and shake well. Pour the drink unstrained into a chilled double rocks glass and garnish with the mint sprig, lime wheel and cinnamon.

CHAI SYRUP

◇ In a small saucepan, bring 6 ounces water to a boil. Remove from the heat, add 2 chai tea bags and let steep for 5 minutes. Discard the tea bags. Stir ¼ cup sugar into the tea until dissolved. Transfer the syrup to a jar and let cool. Refrigerate for up to 2 weeks. Makes about 7 ounces.

M

MANHATTAN

Andrew Pollard · Wirtz Beverage Nevada · Las Vegas

the classic
MANHATTAN

The Manhattan dates back at least to the 1880s; it's typically either rye- or bourbon-based. Andrew Pollard prefers using spicy (ri)1 whiskey or Basil Hayden's bourbon, which has notes of rye.

Ice

1 ounce rye whiskey

1 ounce Carpano Antica Formula or other sweet vermouth

½ teaspoon orange curaçao

2 dashes of Angostura bitters

Fill a pint glass with ice. Add all of the remaining ingredients and stir well. Strain into a chilled coupe.

the twist
SAN GENNARO

This take on the Manhattan is Pollard's tribute to Italian American culture and the annual San Gennaro festival in New York's Little Italy. He combines rye, a quintessentially American spirit, with three from Italy: citrusy Averna amaro, spicy Campari and the sweet vermouth Carpano Antica Formula.

Ice

1 ounce bonded rye whiskey, preferably Rittenhouse 100

1 ounce Averna or Amaro Montenegro

1 ounce Carpano Antica Formula or other sweet vermouth

½ teaspoon Campari

1 or 2 maraschino cherries, preferably Luxardo, for garnish

Fill a pint glass with ice. Add all of the remaining ingredients except the garnish and stir well. Strain into a chilled coupe and garnish with the cherries.

"Abysse" Champagne saucer from Baccarat; "Padova" cocktail fork by Elsa Peretti for Tiffany & Co.

SAN GENNARO

the reinvention
THE MAYAN

When Pollard created this Manhattan variation, his objective was "to take a cocktail that's usually identified as a tough guy's drink and make it approachable." He describes The Mayan as "sweet, spicy, boozy and balanced. Every sip feels like a warm hug." Left-over infused vermouth can be stirred into coffee or poured over vanilla ice cream (any extra chocolate-covered cherries would be good with ice cream, too).

Ice

1½ ounces rye whiskey

1 ounce Amaro Meletti or Amaro Nonino (bittersweet herbal liqueurs)

½ ounce Cinnamon-Fig Vermouth (below)

2 dashes of Angostura bitters

Pinch of cayenne pepper

3 chocolate-covered cherries dusted with cayenne pepper and cinnamon and skewered on a pick, for garnish

Fill a pint glass with ice. Add the rye, amaro, Cinnamon-Fig Vermouth, bitters and cayenne pepper and stir well. Strain into a chilled coupe and garnish the drink with the skewered chocolate-covered cherries.

CINNAMON-FIG VERMOUTH

In a jar, combine 7 ounces sweet vermouth with 2 cinnamon sticks, ½ cup halved dried Black Mission figs and 1 tablespoon sugar. Refrigerate for 48 hours. Strain the infused vermouth into a clean jar and refrigerate for up to 3 weeks. Makes about 5 ounces.

MARGARITA

Ryan Fitzgerald • Beretta • San Francisco

the classic
MARGARITA

According to master mixologist Dale DeGroff, a drink called the Tequila Daisy was served at Tijuana's Agua Caliente racetrack in the 1920s. It was made with lemon juice, tequila and a sweet ingredient—the template for a Margarita.

Ice

1½ ounces blanco tequila

1 ounce Cointreau or other triple sec

¾ ounce fresh lime juice

Fill a cocktail shaker with ice. Add the tequila, Cointreau and fresh lime juice and shake well. Strain the drink into a chilled coupe.

the twist
TOMMY'S MARGARITA

This Margarita riff was created in 1987 by Julio Bermejo at Tommy's Mexican Restaurant in San Francisco. Ryan Fitzgerald argues that replacing orange-flavored triple sec with agave syrup showcases the taste of the tequila—especially aged ones like reposados and añejos.

Ice

2 ounces reposado tequila

1 ounce fresh lime juice

1 ounce agave syrup (1 tablespoon agave nectar mixed with 1 tablespoon water)

Fill a cocktail shaker with ice. Add the tequila, fresh lime juice and agave syrup and shake well. Strain the drink into a chilled, ice-filled double rocks glass.

the reinvention
MEXICO 70

Fitzgerald, who admits to a chronic case of World Cup fever, named this sparkling tequila-lime drink to honor the 1970 World Cup, which was played in Mexico. (Brazil won, led by Pelé.) It's a terrific brunch cocktail.

Ice

- 1 ounce blanco tequila
- ½ ounce fresh lime juice
- ¼ ounce agave nectar
- 3 ounces chilled dry sparkling wine
- 1 lime wheel or lime twist, for garnish

Fill a cocktail shaker with ice. Add the tequila, lime juice and agave nectar and shake well. Fine-strain (P.18) into a chilled flute and top with the sparkling wine. Garnish the drink with the lime wheel.

MARGARITA P.99

MEXICO 70

"Format" Champagne saucer by Rosenthal; "Vertigo" cocktail pick by Christofle; "Patrician" flute by Lobmeyr from Kneen & Co.

MARTINI
BACKSTORY

The most iconic cocktail, the Martini, is also the most protean. The ingredients in the drink can vary so greatly that ordering one always requires a back-and-forth between customer and bartender: "Vodka or gin? Dry or sweet? Shaken or stirred? Olives or a twist?" A 1911 recipe called for equal parts gin and dry vermouth, with a couple of dashes of orange bitters. The most famous Martini drinker, James Bond, liked his made with vodka (shaken, not stirred). Today, at Barcelona's Coctelería Boadas and London's Connaught Hotel, bartenders present Martinis with a Spanish-style "long pour"—straining the drink in a dramatic stream from above their heads into the glass.

MARTINI

Eric Alperin • The Varnish • Los Angeles

the classic
MARTINI

"Most people ask for dry Martinis (made with little or no vermouth) because they've had a bad vermouth experience," says Eric Alperin. "Like wine, vermouth isn't meant to be kept open for months. It should be refrigerated and used within a week."

Ice

2 ounces gin

1 ounce dry vermouth

1 olive or 1 lemon twist, for garnish

Fill a pint glass with ice. Add the gin and vermouth and stir well. Strain into a chilled coupe and garnish with the olive or lemon twist.

the twist
SWEET MARTINI

According to Alperin, very early Martinis were made with gin and sweet, not dry, vermouth. This one, from around 1888, has a sherry-like taste.

Ice

2 ounces gin

1 ounce sweet vermouth

1 brandied cherry, for garnish

Fill a pint glass with ice. Add the gin and vermouth and stir well. Strain into a chilled coupe and garnish the drink with the brandied cherry.

A
B
C
D
E
F
G
H
I
J
K
L
M
N
O
P
Q
R
S
T
U
V
W
X
Y
Z

the reinvention
⟼ CAPRICIOUS

At Tales of the Cocktail 2008, an annual festival in New Orleans, Alperin created this Martini variation for a party hosted by St-Germain, the French producers of artisanal elderflower liqueur. Because vermouth and gin have lots of botanical elements, they're natural partners for the lightly sweet, floral liqueur.

◇ Ice
◇ 1½ ounces gin
◇ ½ ounce St-Germain elderflower liqueur
◇ ½ ounce dry vermouth
◇ 2 dashes of Peychaud's bitters
◇ 1 lemon twist, for garnish

Fill a pint glass with ice. Add the gin, St-Germain elderflower liqueur, dry vermouth and Peychaud's bitters and stir well. Strain into a chilled coupe and garnish the drink with the lemon twist.

CAPRICIOUS

"Patrician" Champagne cup by
Lobmeyr from Kneen & Co.

MICHELADA

Damian Windsor • The Roger Room • Los Angeles

the classic
MICHELADA

"You can make Micheladas with tomato or Clamato juice—everyone has a preference," says Damian Windsor. He makes his version of the Mexican classic with tomato.

◇ Ice
◇ 2 **ounces chilled tomato juice**
◇ 1 **ounce fresh lime juice**
◇ ¾ **ounce Simple Syrup (p. 19)**
◇ 4 **dashes of Maggi seasoning**
  or Worcestershire sauce
◇ 2 **dashes of hot sauce**
◇ 2 **pinches of sea salt**
◇ 12 **ounces chilled lager, preferably Mexican**

◇ Fill a chilled pint glass three-quarters full with ice. Add the tomato and lime juices, Simple Syrup, Maggi seasoning, hot sauce and a pinch of sea salt. Stir well. Add enough lager to fill the glass; top with another pinch of salt. As you finish the drink, continue to pour in more lager.

the twist
MICHELADA SANGRITA

Sangrita, a spicy, citrusy tomato drink, inspired this Michelada variation. To mimic sangrita's flavor, Windsor replaced the Michelada's simple syrup with grenadine.

Ice

2 ounces chilled tomato juice

2 ounces fresh lime juice

1 ounce grenadine, preferably homemade (p. 19)

4 dashes of Maggi seasoning
or Worcestershire sauce

2 dashes of hot sauce

2 pinches of sea salt

12 ounces chilled lager, preferably Mexican

Fill a chilled pint glass three-quarters full with ice. Add the tomato and lime juices, grenadine, Maggi seasoning, hot sauce and a pinch of sea salt. Stir well. Add enough lager to fill the glass, then top with another pinch of salt. As you finish the drink, continue to pour in more lager.

the reinvention
MICHELADA GINGEMBRE

Windsor's favorite low-alcohol cocktail had been the Shandygaff (citrus soda mixed with lager) until he created a version with fresh ginger juice and a hoppy IPA; it was delicious. Adding a dash of hot sauce made the drink even better.

Ice

6 ounces chilled Sprite

1 ounce fresh lemon juice

1 ounce Simple Syrup (p. 19)

¾ ounce fresh ginger juice
(grated from a 2-inch piece of fresh ginger and pressed through a fine strainer)

Dash of jalapeño hot sauce

12 ounces chilled IPA-style beer

Pinch of sea salt

Fill a chilled pint glass halfway with ice. Add the Sprite, lemon juice, Simple Syrup, ginger juice and hot sauce; stir well. Add enough beer to fill the glass; top with the salt. As you finish the drink, continue to pour in more beer.

MICHELADA GINGEMBRE

"Iskender" shot glass by Hermès;
"Vesta" glass by William Yeoward.

MOJITO

Ryan Maybee • Manifesto • Kansas City, MO

the classic
MOJITO

Although there have been versions of this rum-mint cocktail in Cuba since the late 1800s, it became an international sensation when Ernest Hemingway endorsed the Mojitos at La Bodeguita del Medio in Havana. Still, the drink didn't make its way into American bars until the 1960s, when it was served at New York's legendary La Fonda del Sol.

5   mint leaves, plus 1 mint sprig for garnish
1½   ounces chilled club soda
Ice
1½   ounces white rum
¾   ounce fresh lime juice
¾   ounce Simple Syrup (p. 19)

In a collins glass, muddle the mint leaves with ½ ounce of the soda. Add ice. Fill a cocktail shaker with ice. Add the rum, lime juice and Simple Syrup; shake well. Strain into the glass. Add the remaining soda and the mint sprig.

the twist
MOJO ROYALE

Ryan Maybee loves tarragon's licorice flavor, so he decided to use the herb in place of the mint in a Mojito. Then he swapped out the rum for cachaça (to get more kick) and added sparkling wine to keep the drink refreshing. He opts for brut cava in his Mojo Royale.

8   tarragon leaves, plus 1 tarragon sprig for garnish
½   ounce chilled club soda
Ice
1½   ounces cachaça
¾   ounce fresh lime juice
¾   ounce Simple Syrup (p. 19)
2   ounces chilled dry sparkling wine
4   dashes of Angostura bitters

In a shaker, muddle the tarragon leaves and soda. Add ice, the cachaça, lime juice and syrup; shake. Fine-strain (**P.18**) into a wineglass. Add the wine, bitters and sprig.

MOJO ROYALE

THE DRAKE'S RETURN P.112

"Simplicity" glass by Varga from Tabula Tua; coupe from Leo Design.

the reinvention

THE DRAKE'S RETURN

MAKES 4 DRINKS

For his deconstructed, gin-spiked Mojito, Maybee tops the drink with a minty, limey foam. "The key to a good foam is to use a stabilizer such as egg whites and to keep the canister chilled," he says. Maybee flavors the cocktail with hibiscus-rose bitters (available at absmebybitteringco.com), but in a pinch, Peychaud's bitters will do.

- **20 mint leaves**
- **2 teaspoons Simple Syrup (p. 19)**
- **6 ounces aged rum, preferably Ron Zacapa 23**
- **3 ounces gin, preferably Tanqueray Rangpur**
- **8 dashes of hibiscus-rose bitters**
- **Ice**
- **Citrus-Mint Foam (below)**

In a pint glass, lightly muddle 16 mint leaves with the Simple Syrup. Add the rum, gin, bitters and ice and stir well. Fine-strain (**P.18**) into 4 chilled coupes and top with the Citrus-Mint Foam. Garnish each drink with a mint leaf.

CITRUS-MINT FOAM

In the canister of a cream whipper (see Note), combine 1 ounce orange curaçao, 3 ounces Simple Syrup (**P.19**), 2 ounces fresh lime juice, 1 large egg white and 4 mint leaves. Seal the canister, shake hard and charge twice according to the manufacturer's directions, using 1 or 2 nitrous oxide chargers; shake well between charges. Refrigerate for 1 hour. Shake before using. Makes enough foam for 4 drinks.

NOTE Cream whippers and nitrous oxide chargers are sold at kitchenware shops and *surlatable.com*.

■ the mocktail
MOCK MOJITO MULE

Maybee fuses the flavors of two classic cocktails— the Mojito and the Moscow Mule (vodka, ginger beer and lime)—in this citrusy, ginger-spiked drink. Since there are so many ginger beers on the market (some good and some not so good), Maybee prepares his own using homemade ginger syrup and tonic water.

½ **lime, quartered**
2 **orange wedges**
1 **ounce Ginger Syrup (below)**
Ice cubes, plus crushed ice
5 **mint leaves, plus 1 mint sprig for garnish**
2 **ounces chilled tonic water**

In a cocktail shaker, muddle the lime quarters and orange wedges with the Ginger Syrup. Add ice cubes and the mint leaves and shake well. Fine-strain (**P.18**) into a chilled, crushed ice–filled collins glass. Stir in the tonic water and garnish with the mint sprig.

GINGER SYRUP

In a small saucepan, combine ½ cup sugar with 4 ounces water. Simmer over moderate heat, stirring, until the sugar dissolves. Add ⅓ cup minced fresh ginger; simmer over low heat for 30 minutes, stirring occasionally. Let cool, then pour the syrup through a fine strainer into a jar. Refrigerate for up to 2 weeks. Makes about 5 ounces.

A B C D E F G H I J K L M N O P Q R S T U V W X Y Z

NEGRONI

Jacques Bezuidenhout · Fifth Floor · San Francisco

NEGRONI

*Tumbler by Adolf Loos for Lobmeyr
from Neue Galerie.*

the classic
NEGRONI

The Negroni was invented in 1925 when Florentine count Camillo Negroni asked a bartender to make his Americano (a mixture of Campari, sweet vermouth and club soda) with gin instead of soda.

◇ Ice
◇ 1 ounce each of Campari, London dry gin and sweet vermouth
◇ 1 or 2 orange wheels, for garnish

◇ Fill a chilled rocks glass with ice. Add the Campari, gin and vermouth; stir well. Garnish with the orange wheels.

the twist
TEQUILA NEGRONI

A huge tequila fan, Jacques Bezuidenhout wanted to try the spirit in one of his favorite classic cocktails, the Negroni. Bold, agave-forward blanco tequila turned out to be delicious with Campari's earthy flavors.

◇ Ice
◇ 1 ounce each of Campari, blanco tequila and sweet vermouth
◇ 1 orange wheel, for garnish

◇ Fill a chilled rocks glass with ice. Add the Campari, tequila and vermouth; stir well. Garnish with the orange wheel.

the reinvention
SPANISH NEGRONI

Bezuidenhout created this drink for SF Chefs 2011, an annual food, wine and spirits festival in San Francisco. To make the Negroni more food-friendly, he spiked it with nutty amontillado sherry. He thinks the result would be great with jamón—dry-cured Spanish ham—and a little bread and olive oil.

◇ Ice
◇ 1½ ounces amontillado sherry
◇ 1 ounce each of Campari and London dry gin
◇ ½ ounce sweet vermouth
◇ 1 orange twist, for garnish

◇ Fill a pint glass with ice. Add the sherry, Campari, gin and vermouth and stir well. Strain into a chilled coupe and garnish with the orange twist.

OLD-FASHIONED

Anthony Schmidt · Noble Experiment · San Diego

the classic
■ OLD-FASHIONED

According to cocktail historian David Wondrich, the Old-Fashioned is a direct descendant of the earliest cocktail, which in the early 1800s consisted of "a little water, a little sugar, a lot of liquor, and a couple splashes of bitters."

1 **sugar cube**

3 **dashes of Angostura bitters**

¼ **ounce chilled club soda**

Ice

2 **ounces bourbon**

1 **lemon or orange twist, for garnish**

In a chilled rocks glass, combine the sugar cube, bitters and club soda and muddle to a paste. Add ice and the bourbon and stir well. Garnish with the twist.

the twist
■ MONACO FRIAR

One of Anthony Schmidt's favorite drinks is the Monaco Friar. "I love how the honey and herbal qualities of the Bénédictine pair with a fine Scotch," he says. "It's a perfect drink during the colder months."

Ice

2 **ounces Scotch**

½ **ounce Bénédictine (brandy-based herbal liqueur)**

3 **dashes of Angostura bitters**

1 **lemon twist, for garnish**

Fill a chilled rocks glass with ice. Add the Scotch, Bénédictine and bitters; stir well. Garnish with the lemon twist.

MONACO FRIAR

"Legin" glass from Moser.

the reinvention

AMERICAN-STYLE OLD-FASHIONED

■

Bartenders have been infusing whiskey and bourbon with bacon for years. Schmidt and his mentor, Sam Ross, have taken to combining the meat with Angostura bitters. Schmidt thinks that the bacon-infused bitters add a "controlled complexity" to this Old-Fashioned without making it too salty or "hammy."

◇ **1 brown sugar cube**
◇ **3 to 4 dashes of Baco-Stura Bitters (below)**
◇ **1 teaspoon chilled club soda**
◇ **Ice**
◇ **1 ounce bonded rye whiskey**
◇ **1 ounce Laird's bonded apple brandy**
◇ **1 orange twist, flamed (p. 18), for garnish**

◇ In a chilled rocks glass, combine the sugar cube, Baco-Stura Bitters and club soda and muddle to a paste. Add ice and the whiskey and brandy and stir well. Garnish the drink with the flamed orange twist.

BACO-STURA BITTERS

◇ In a skillet, cook 3 thick-cut strips of bacon until crisp. Pour 7½ ounces Angostura bitters into a large jar. Add the bacon and all the fat to the jar. Add ½ ounce Angostura bitters to the skillet and cook over moderate heat to deglaze the skillet, scraping up any browned bits; add to the jar. Let cool, then seal tightly and freeze for 24 hours. Spoon off the solidified fat and strain the bitters through a coffee filter into a clean jar. Keep at room temperature for up to 1 month. Makes about 6 ounces.

PIMM'S CUP

Greg Best · Holeman & Finch Public House · Atlanta

the classic
PIMM'S CUP

Wimbledon spectators drink ten to fifteen thousand Pimm's Cups every day. Americans often make the low-alcohol cocktail with Sprite or 7-Up, but Greg Best opts for the British way, using bitter lemon soda for "the perfect balance between sweet and tart."

Ice

- **2 ounces Pimm's No. 1 (gin-based aperitif)**
- **4 ounces chilled bitter lemon soda (see Note)**
- **1 lemon wedge, 1 apple slice and 1 cucumber spear, for garnish**

Fill a chilled collins glass with ice. Add the Pimm's and lemon soda and stir well. Garnish with the lemon wedge, apple slice and cucumber spear.

NOTE Schweppes and Fever-Tree make high-quality, widely available bitter lemon sodas.

the twist
H&F HOUSE PIMM'S CUP

Best calls New Orleans "the American hometown of the Pimm's Cup." (The city's 200-year-old Napoleon House is known for its version of the drink.) Paying homage to this heritage, Best flavors this ginger ale–based riff on the drink with Peychaud's bitters, another New Orleans signature.

Ice

- **2 ounces Pimm's No. 1**
- **1 ounce chilled lemonade, preferably homemade**
- **2 dashes of Peychaud's bitters**
- **3 ounces chilled ginger ale**
- **2 cucumber wheels**
- **1 large mint sprig, for garnish**

Fill a chilled collins glass with ice. Add the Pimm's, lemonade and bitters; stir well. Stir in the ginger ale. Submerge the cucumber in the drink; garnish with the mint.

the reinvention
PIMM'S CUP ROYALE

According to Best, the Royale was created during "an intense brunch service" at Holeman & Finch. "A newly married couple was telling us how they loved the Pimm's Cup but had to drink too many to get that 'brunchy, buzzy' feeling." Determined to keep the balance of the classic while pleasing his guests, Best added Cognac, peach liqueur and Champagne.

Ice

1½ ounces Pimm's No. 1

½ ounce VSOP Cognac

½ teaspoon crème de pêche or other peach liqueur

1 ounce chilled lemonade, preferably homemade

Dash of Peychaud's bitters

Dash of orange bitters

3½ ounces chilled brut Champagne
    or dry sparkling wine

1 large basil sprig and 1 cucumber spear,
    for garnish

Fill a chilled collins glass with ice. Add the Pimm's, Cognac, crème de pêche, lemonade and bitters; stir well. Stir in the Champagne; garnish with the basil and cucumber.

the mocktail
LYNN'S CUP

"This mocktail was a collaborative effort between a 'slightly dehydrated' barkeep and a pregnant woman," says Best. It's light, delicate and similar in appearance to a Pimm's Cup, but prettier—pink-hued and flecked with bits of strawberry, basil and cucumber.

2 cucumber wheels

1 strawberry, sliced

5 basil leaves

Ice

1 ounce fresh lemon juice

1 ounce chilled Earl Grey syrup (¾ ounce brewed
    Earl Grey tea mixed with 1½ tablespoons sugar)

4 ounces chilled ginger ale

1 lemon twist and 1 mint sprig, for garnish

In a chilled collins glass, muddle the cucumber, strawberry and basil. Add ice and the lemon juice, Earl Grey syrup and ginger ale; stir well. Garnish with the lemon twist and mint sprig.

PIMM'S CUP ROYALE

"Smoke" glass by Arnolfo di Cambio from Fitzsu.

PISCO PUNCH

Erik Adkins · The Slanted Door · San Francisco

¶ the classic
PISCO PUNCH

MAKES ABOUT 12 DRINKS

Duncan Nicol, owner of San Francisco's legendary Bank Exchange bar, invented the Pisco Punch in the late 1800s. One of the drink's key ingredients, pineapple gum syrup, went out of production long ago and became available again only recently.

- 24 ounces pisco
- 8 ounces fresh lemon juice (from about 6 lemons)
- 8 ounces water
- One 8½-fluid-ounce bottle pineapple gum syrup (see Note)
- 2½ cups fresh pineapple chunks
- Ice, preferably 1 large block (p. 18)
- Thin pineapple slices, for garnish

In a punch bowl, combine the pisco, lemon juice, water, gum syrup and pineapple chunks and refrigerate until chilled, about 2 hours. Add ice. Serve the punch in chilled coupes and garnish with the pineapple slices.

NOTE Pineapple gum syrup, thickened pineapple-flavored simple syrup, is available at *smallhandfoods.com*.

"Mitos" coupes from Ameico; pitcher by Lobmeyr from Neue Galerie; vase by Rosenthal from The End of History.

PISCO PUNCH

the twist
PISCO-APRICOT TROPICÁL

Certainly inspired by the Pisco Punch, the Pisco-Apricot Tropicál first appeared in Charles H. Baker's 1951 South American Gentleman's Companion. *Erik Adkins thought the recipe could be better, so he replaced its watery pineapple juice with pineapple gum syrup.*

Ice
1½ ounces pisco
½ ounce apricot brandy
¾ ounce fresh lemon juice
¾ ounce pineapple gum syrup (see Note, p. 122)
2 dashes of Angostura bitters

Fill a cocktail shaker with ice. Add all of the remaining ingredients and shake well. Strain into a chilled coupe.

the reinvention
SAN FRANCISCO FIZZ

"This drink is kind of a mash-up of the Pisco Punch, the Mai Tai and the Silver Fizz," says Adkins. The orgeat and lime come from the Mai Tai, the club soda and egg white from the Silver Fizz.

2 ounces pisco
1 ounce fresh lime juice
½ ounce pineapple gum syrup (see Note, p. 122)
½ ounce orgeat (almond-flavored syrup)
1 large egg white
Ice
2 ounces chilled club soda

In a cocktail shaker, combine the pisco, lime juice, gum syrup, orgeat and egg white and shake well. Add ice and shake again. Pour 1 ounce of the club soda into a chilled collins glass. Strain the drink into the glass, then stir in the remaining 1 ounce of club soda.

PISCO SOUR

Linden Pride · Saxon & Parole · New York City

the classic
PISCO SOUR

The Pisco Sour, a Whiskey Sour variation, was invented by Victor Morris in Lima, Peru, in the early 1900s. He likely used lime juice, but most Pisco Sours today use lemon. Shaking the drink first without ice (a.k.a. dry-shaking) emulsifies the egg white and gives the drink an airy texture.

◇ 1½ ounces pisco
◇ 1 ounce fresh lemon juice
◇ 1 ounce Simple Syrup (p. 19)
◇ 1 large egg white
◇ Ice
◇ 3 drops of Angostura bitters, for garnish

◇ In a shaker, combine the pisco, lemon juice, Simple Syrup and egg white; shake well. Add ice; shake again. Fine-strain (**P.18**) into a chilled wineglass; dot with the bitters.

the twist
SALTED MAPLE

Linden Pride created this autumnal Pisco Sour riff for the inaugural drink list at Neil Perry's modern Asian restaurant Spice Temple in Sydney. Pride uses grade B maple syrup to give the sweet-savory cocktail a deep, rich flavor.

◇ Ice
◇ 1½ ounces pisco
◇ 1 ounce fresh lemon juice
◇ ½ ounce pure maple syrup
◇ ½ ounce Simple Syrup (p. 19)
◇ Pinch of salt
◇ 2 drops of Angostura bitters and 1 drop of Peychaud's bitters, for garnish

◇ Fill a cocktail shaker with ice. Add the pisco, lemon juice, maple syrup, Simple Syrup and salt; shake well. Strain into a chilled wineglass, then dot with the bitters.

the reinvention

CUCUMBER, SALT & SMOKE

Mezcal, made from fire-roasted agave, provides the smokiness in this unusual Pisco Sour update. The cucumber is fresh and herbaceous, and even though the cocktail contains simple syrup, a pinch of salt makes it more dry than sweet. While the shaken egg white adds a dramatic foamy head, the drink is equally delicious without an egg white.

One 1-inch cucumber slice, chopped
1 ounce pisco
1 ounce mezcal
1 ounce fresh lemon juice
1 ounce Simple Syrup (p. 19)
1 large egg white
Pinch of salt
Ice
3 drops of Peychaud's bitters, for garnish

In a cocktail shaker, muddle the cucumber. Add the pisco, mezcal, lemon juice, Simple Syrup, egg white and salt and shake well. Add ice and shake again. Fine-strain (P.18) into a chilled wineglass. Dot the drink with the Peychaud's bitters and swirl decoratively.

CUCUMBER, SALT & SMOKE

"Globe" glass from Scandinavian Design Center.

QUEEN'S PARK SWIZZLE

Thad Vogler · Bar Agricole · San Francisco

the classic
QUEEN'S PARK SWIZZLE

Born at Trinidad's now-closed Queen's Park Hotel, this early-1900s lime-rum cocktail is traditionally served over crushed ice and mixed with a swizzle stick to stir the drink without creating bubbles. Innovative bars such as NYC's Milk & Honey use "pebble" ice (pictured at right) for crushed-ice cocktails because it melts more slowly, diluting drinks less quickly.

2 ounces dark rum, preferably aged Demerara rum, such as El Dorado 15-Year-Old Special Reserve

1 ounce fresh lime juice

½ ounce Rich Simple Syrup (p. 19)

Crushed ice

3 dashes of Angostura bitters and 1 mint sprig, for garnish

In a chilled collins glass, combine the rum, lime juice and Rich Simple Syrup. Add crushed ice. Spin a swizzle stick or bar spoon between your hands to mix the drink, then add more crushed ice. Top with the bitters and garnish with the mint sprig.

"L'Alba Rossa" glass by Carlo Moretti from Moss; "Murano" bowl from The End of History.

QUEEN'S PARK SWIZZLE

the twist
QUEEN'S PARK JULEP

The Mint Julep (bourbon, simple syrup, crushed ice and mint sprigs) inspired this Queen's Park Swizzle twist. "The rich sweetness of bourbon makes it a natural substitute for Demerara rum," says Thad Vogler.

2 **ounces bourbon**
1 **ounce fresh lime juice**
½ **ounce Rich Simple Syrup (p. 19)**
Crushed ice
5 **dashes of Angostura bitters and 1 mint sprig, for garnish**

In a chilled collins glass, combine the bourbon, lime juice and Rich Simple Syrup. Add crushed ice. Spin a swizzle stick or bar spoon between your hands to mix the drink, then add more crushed ice. Top with the bitters, garnish with the mint sprig and serve with a metal spoon-straw.

the reinvention
DOLORES PARK SWIZZLE

Vogler created this cocktail for the late-night lounge Beretta in San Francisco, where all the drinks are variations on classics. Aromatic West Indian rhum agricole stands in for the Demerara rum in the Queen's Park Swizzle; cane syrup and maraschino liqueur add richness.

2 **ounces white rhum agricole**
¼ **ounce maraschino liqueur**
½ **teaspoon absinthe**
1 **ounce fresh lime juice**
½ **ounce cane syrup (see Note)**
Crushed ice
4 **dashes of Peychaud's bitters and 1 or 2 mint sprigs, for garnish**

In a chilled collins glass, combine all of the ingredients except the ice and garnishes. Add crushed ice. Spin a swizzle stick or bar spoon between your hands to mix the drink; add more crushed ice. Top with the bitters and mint.
NOTE Sweet, thick cane syrup is available at Whole Foods and *cocktailkingdom.com.*

the mocktail
FREE JAMAICA

Fresh ginger juice replaces the classic rum in this tasty, alcohol-free swizzle. Hibiscus tea, sold as flor de Jamaica in Latin markets, tops the drink, creating the red tint that normally comes from Peychaud's bitters.

4 ounces water

2 tablespoons dried hibiscus flowers or loose hibiscus tea

½ ounce fresh ginger juice (grated from a 2-inch piece of fresh ginger and pressed through a fine strainer)

1 ounce fresh lime juice

½ ounce Rich Simple Syrup (p. 19)

Crushed ice

1 or 2 mint sprigs, for garnish

1. In a small saucepan, bring the water to a boil. Remove from the heat, add the hibiscus flowers and let steep for 20 minutes. Strain and let cool completely.

2. In a chilled collins glass, combine the ginger juice, lime juice and Rich Simple Syrup. Add crushed ice. Spin a swizzle stick or bar spoon between your hands to mix the drink, then add more crushed ice. Top with the cooled hibiscus tea, garnish with mint sprigs and serve the drink with a metal spoon-straw.

PROFILE OF A FIZZ

A fizz is a sour (combining a spirit, citrus and a sweetener) topped with an effervescent ingredient such as club soda or Champagne and typically served without ice. Tailor-made for refreshment, these cocktails were originally consumed for hydration, hence the lack of elaborate garnish (which would slow down drinking). The most famous fizz of all is the Ramos Gin Fizz, created in the late 19th century at Henry Ramos's Imperial Cabinet Saloon in New Orleans. The cocktail includes an egg white, which not only adds protein but also, when shaken, creates a wonderful airy texture. The freshest eggs produce the smallest bubbles, resulting in an exceptionally light drink.

RAMOS GIN FIZZ

Rhiannon Enlil · Cure · New Orleans

the classic
RAMOS GIN FIZZ

There are several classic recipes for the Ramos Gin Fizz. Rhiannon Enlil prefers a "creamier, boozier and more floral" one to the lighter version published in the 1928 New Orleans Item-Tribune by bartender Henry Charles Ramos. Enlil agrees with Ramos, however, that you must "shake and shake and shake until there is not a bubble left but the drink is smooth and snowy white and the consistency of good rich milk."

- ¾ ounce fresh lemon juice
- 1 large egg white
- Ice
- 2 ounces gin, preferably Plymouth
- 1½ ounces chilled heavy cream
- 1 ounce Simple Syrup (p. 19)
- 8 drops of orange flower water
- 1½ ounces chilled club soda
- 1 orange twist, for garnish

In a cocktail shaker, combine the lemon juice and egg white and shake well. Add ice and the gin, heavy cream, Simple Syrup and orange flower water and shake again. Pour the club soda into a chilled collins glass, then slowly strain the drink into the glass. Garnish with the orange twist and serve with a straw.

the twist
GINGER BAKER FIZZ

Enlil uses the unlikely but terrific combination of crème de cacao and ginger liqueur in place of the classic drink's simple syrup. She also omits the orange flower water and subs out the club soda for cold ginger beer.

¾ ounce fresh lemon juice

1 large egg white

Ice

2 ounces gin, preferably Plymouth

½ ounce crème de cacao

½ ounce ginger liqueur

1½ ounces chilled heavy cream

1½ ounces chilled ginger beer

1 orange twist, for garnish

In a cocktail shaker, combine the lemon juice and egg white and shake well. Add ice and the gin, crème de cacao, ginger liqueur and heavy cream and shake again. Pour the ginger beer into a chilled collins glass, then slowly strain the drink into the glass. Garnish with the orange twist and serve with a straw.

GINGER BAKER FIZZ

"Revolution" liqueur glass
by Felicia Ferrone.

the reinvention
RUM JULIUS

Inspired by the Orange Julius, the famous orangey milkshake, Enlil flavors this rum drink with a quick homemade vanilla syrup. Leftover syrup can be stirred into club soda, hot chocolate or coffee, or used for milkshakes.

¾ ounce fresh orange juice
½ ounce fresh lemon juice
1 large egg white
Ice
2 ounces aged rum
1 ounce chilled heavy cream
¾ ounce Vanilla Syrup (below)
3 drops of orange flower water
2 dashes of orange bitters
1½ ounces chilled club soda

In a cocktail shaker, combine the orange juice, lemon juice and egg white and shake well. Add ice and the rum, heavy cream, Vanilla Syrup, orange flower water and bitters and shake again. Pour the club soda into a chilled collins glass, then slowly strain the drink into the glass. Serve with a straw.

VANILLA SYRUP

In a small saucepan, bring 4 ounces water to a simmer. Remove from the heat, add ½ split vanilla bean and let steep for 20 minutes. Strain the liquid into a jar and stir in ½ cup sugar. Refrigerate the syrup for up to 2 weeks. Makes about 6 ounces.

RUSTY NAIL

Anu Apte · Rob Roy · Seattle

the classic

RUSTY NAIL

This is Anu Apte's recipe for a classic Rusty Nail: a 1:1 Scotch–Drambuie ratio. Since Drambuie is quite sweet, though, Apte sometimes uses 2 ounces of Scotch and ½ to ¾ ounce of honey liqueur. "People should experiment with ratios," she says.

Ice
1   ounce blended Scotch
1   ounce Drambuie
     (honeyed Scotch-based liqueur)
1   lemon twist, for garnish

Fill a chilled rocks glass three-quarters full with ice. Add the Scotch and Drambuie and stir well. Garnish the drink with the lemon twist.

the twist
BITTERED SWEETS

"Seattle is known for liking bitter flavors," says Apte. "Adding a dash of orange bitters to the Rusty Nail suits the place."

Ice
2   ounces blended Scotch
½   ounce Drambuie
     (honeyed Scotch-based liqueur)
Dash of orange bitters
1   orange twist, for garnish

Fill a pint glass with ice. Add the Scotch, Drambuie and bitters and stir well. Strain into chilled coupe and garnish with the orange twist.

the reinvention

AINSLEY, HERE IS YOUR MEADOW

Upon tasting her frothy, smoky, lemony riff on a Rusty Nail, Apte says, "I felt like I was standing in a meadow in Scotland breathing in fresh air. The aroma is earthy yet light, and the drink isn't as heavy as the original." It's a great brunch drink.

1½ ounces smoky single-malt Scotch, such as Islay

1 ounce Drambuie (honeyed Scotch-based liqueur)

¾ ounce fresh lemon juice

1 large egg white

Ice

1 ounce bitter lemon soda (see Note, p. 119)

1 whole clove and a tiny pinch of saffron threads, for garnish

In a cocktail shaker, combine the Scotch, Drambuie, lemon juice and egg white and shake well. Add ice and shake again. Strain into a chilled collins glass. Slowly pour in the lemon soda and garnish with the clove and saffron.

the mocktail

RUSTY 2-60D

Thanks to Lapsang souchong tea, this iced drink is smoky and refreshing at the same time. It's delicious hot or cold.

6 ounces boiling water

1 tablespoon Lapsang souchong tea leaves

5 saffron threads

2 whole cloves

1 tablespoon honey

Ice

1 lemon wedge, for garnish

In a heatproof measuring cup, combine the water, tea leaves, saffron and cloves. Let steep for 8 minutes. Stir in the honey until dissolved. Strain and let cool. Pour the drink into a chilled, ice-filled collins glass and garnish with the lemon wedge.

AINSLEY, HERE IS YOUR MEADOW

"Alana Essence" highball glass by Waterford; liqueur glass by Karl Lagerfeld for Orrefors.

SANGRIA

Bridget Albert · Southern Wine & Spirits · Chicago

RED SANGRIA P.142

"Kartio" thin tumblers by Iittala.

the classic
RED SANGRIA

MAKES 6 DRINKS

Although Spaniards and Portuguese have been drinking sangria for centuries, the brandy-spiked drink didn't make an official appearance in the United States until 1964, at the World's Fair in New York City.

One 750-milliliter bottle fruity red wine, such as Merlot

4 ounces brandy

3 ounces Simple Syrup (p. 19)

1 cup mixed chunks of seeded oranges, lemons and limes

Ice

In a pitcher, combine the red wine, brandy, Simple Syrup and fruit. Refrigerate until the drink is chilled and the flavors are blended, 4 to 8 hours. Serve the sangria in chilled, ice-filled wineglasses.

the classic
WHITE SANGRIA

MAKES 6 DRINKS

Bridget Albert usually serves red sangria at night. She opts for white sangria, which is lighter and more refreshing, at brunch and daytime parties like showers and summer barbecues.

One 750-milliliter bottle rich white wine, such as Chardonnay

4 ounces brandy

2 ounces Simple Syrup (p. 19)

1 cup mixed chunks of seeded oranges, lemons and limes

Ice

In a pitcher, combine the white wine, brandy, Simple Syrup and fruit. Refrigerate until the drink is chilled and the flavors are blended, 4 to 8 hours. Serve the sangria in chilled, ice-filled wineglasses.

the twist
SANGRIA TORCIDO

This pretty, copper-colored cocktail is basically white sangria mixed with a fruity Cognac infusion. Albert likes making the drink with Riesling instead of Chardonnay because it's more aromatic and often has hints of pear, grapefruit and apple.

Ice

3 ounces chilled Riesling

2 ounces Fruity Cognac (below)

1 orange wheel, 1 lemon wheel and 1 lime wheel, for garnish

Fill a chilled wineglass with ice. Add the Riesling and Fruity Cognac and stir well. Garnish the drink with the orange, lemon and lime wheels.

FRUITY COGNAC

In a jar, combine half of a 750-milliliter bottle of Cognac with 3 cups sliced strawberries and 2½ cups cubed fresh pineapple. Let macerate at room temperature for 48 hours. Strain the infused Cognac into a clean jar and refrigerate for up to 1 week. Makes about 12 ounces.

the reinvention
SANGRIA COSECHA

Combining cava with figgy, nutty East India sherry and a touch of cinnamon syrup, Albert's robust Sangria Cosecha (Harvest Sangria) is a terrific cold-weather cocktail. To lighten it, just add more sparkling wine.

Ice

4 ounces chilled sparkling white wine, preferably cava

2 ounces East India sherry, preferably Lustau Solera

¼ ounce Cinnamon Syrup (p. 172)

1 orange wheel, 1 lemon wheel, 1 lime wheel and ½ teaspoon golden raisins, for garnish

Fill a chilled wineglass with ice. Add the sparkling wine, sherry and Cinnamon Syrup and stir well. Garnish with the orange, lemon and lime wheels and the golden raisins.

SAZERAC

Mike Ryan • Sable Kitchen & Bar • Chicago

the classic
■ SAZERAC

"This drink was originally made with Cognac," says Mike Ryan. "But after the grape-killing phylloxera epidemic in France all but wiped out Cognac production in the 1870s, bartenders replaced it with American-made rye whiskey." The recipe here is for the "modern" (rye-based) Sazerac.

◇ ¼ ounce absinthe
◇ Ice
◇ 2 ounces bonded rye whiskey, preferably Rittenhouse 100
◇ ½ teaspoon Rich Simple Syrup (p. 19)
◇ 3 dashes of Peychaud's bitters
◇ 1 lemon twist

◇ Rinse a chilled rocks glass with the absinthe and pour out the excess. Fill a pint glass with ice. Add the whiskey, Rich Simple Syrup and Peychaud's bitters and stir well. Strain the drink into the prepared rocks glass, pinch the twist over the drink and discard the twist.

"Mille Nuits" tumbler by Baccarat.

SAZERAC

the twist
PRESCRIPTION SAZERAC

In this basic Sazerac variation, Ryan supplements the rye with Cognac, adding a layer of fruity complexity (Cognac is made from grapes).

- ¼ ounce absinthe
- Ice
- 1 ounce bonded rye whiskey, preferably Rittenhouse 100
- 1 ounce VSOP Cognac
- ¼ ounce Rich Simple Syrup (p. 19)
- 3 dashes of Peychaud's bitters
- 1 lemon twist

Rinse a chilled rocks glass with the absinthe; pour out the excess. Fill a pint glass with ice. Add the rye, Cognac, Rich Simple Syrup and bitters and stir well. Strain into the rocks glass, pinch the twist over the drink and discard.

the reinvention
LORD BULLINGDON'S REVENGE

Ryan created this drink after reading William Thackeray's The Luck of Barry Lyndon and watching Stanley Kubrick's film version of the novel. In the story, the character Lord Bullingdon wounds Lyndon in the leg in a duel. "The Scotch echoes the smoke from the old-style pistols they used," says Ryan. "Chartreuse represents the medicinal herbs used in the poultice for Lyndon's leg."

- ¼ ounce green Chartreuse
- Ice
- 1 ounce blended Scotch
- 1 ounce smoky single-malt Scotch
- ¼ ounce crème de cacao
- Dash of Angostura bitters
- Dash of Fee Brothers Old Fashion aromatic bitters
- 1 lemon twist

Rinse a chilled rocks glass with the Chartreuse; pour out the excess. Fill a pint glass with ice. Add both Scotches, the crème de cacao and both bitters; stir well. Strain into the rocks glass, pinch the twist over the drink and discard.

SHERRY COBBLER

Naomi Schimek • The Spare Room • Los Angeles

the classic
SHERRY COBBLER

According to Naomi Schimek, this Sherry Cobbler was adapted from the one in Harry Johnson's 1882 Bartenders' Manual, in which he declared the fortified-wine cocktail to be "without doubt the most popular beverage in the country, with ladies as well as with gentlemen."

◇ 1 long strip of lemon zest
◇ 1½ teaspoons superfine sugar
◇ Crushed ice
◇ 3 ounces fino sherry
◇ Citrus fruit slices and fresh berries, for garnish

◇ In a pint glass, muddle the lemon zest with the sugar. Add crushed ice and the sherry and stir well. Pour into a chilled wineglass and garnish with fruit.

the twist
SPARE ROOM COBBLER

In the summer, this fruity drink is the house cocktail at the Spare Room. "Wild California strawberries pair really well with sherry, and Cognac adds body and depth," says Schimek.

◇ 4 strawberries
◇ 1 lemon wedge
◇ Crushed ice
◇ 2 ounces fino sherry
◇ ¾ ounce Cognac
◇ ¾ ounce Simple Syrup (p. 19)

◇ In a pint glass, muddle 3 strawberries with the lemon wedge. Add crushed ice and the sherry, Cognac and Simple Syrup and stir well. Pour into a chilled wineglass and garnish with the remaining strawberry.

the reinvention
TEA AT THREE

This blackberry-and-herb-flavored cobbler is bracing, with black tea–infused gin adding a pleasantly tannic bite.

- 5 blackberries
- 1 lemon wedge
- 2 ounces amontillado sherry
- 1 ounce Black Tea Gin (below)
- ¾ ounce Simple Syrup (p. 19)
- Crushed ice
- 1 thyme sprig and 1 lavender sprig, for garnish

In a pint glass, muddle 4 blackberries with the lemon wedge. Add the sherry, Black Tea Gin, Simple Syrup and crushed ice and stir well. Pour into a chilled wineglass and garnish the drink with the remaining blackberry and the thyme and lavender sprigs.

BLACK TEA GIN
In a jar, cover 1 teaspoon black tea leaves or 1 tea bag with 4 ounces gin. Let steep for 2 hours, stirring occasionally. Pour the infused gin through a fine strainer into a clean jar and store at room temperature for up to 1 month. Makes 4 ounces.

TEA AT THREE

"Bellport" goblet by Kate Spade
New York.

SIDECAR

Jonny Raglin · Comstock Saloon · San Francisco

the classic
SIDECAR

According to cocktail expert Dale DeGroff, the Sidecar—said to be invented in the 1930s—is an update of a much older drink called the Brandy Crusta (P.48). While many bartenders consider the sugar rim essential to both drinks, Jonny Raglin asks people their preference. "If no rim, then I simply garnish the drink with a twist."

◇ **Ice**
◇ **1¾ ounces VSOP Cognac**
◇ **¾ ounce orange curaçao**
◇ **¾ ounce fresh lemon juice**
◇ **¼ ounce Simple Syrup (p. 19)**
◇ **Dash of orange bitters**
◇ **1 orange twist, for garnish**

◇ Fill a cocktail shaker with ice. Add all of the remaining ingredients except the garnish and shake well. Strain into a chilled coupe and garnish with the orange twist.

the twist
CHERRY SLIDECAR

Cherry bitters, cherry liqueur and a brandied cherry flavor Raglin's favorite Sidecar variation. At Comstock, he makes the drink with pickled cherry bitters concocted by his business partner and "resident mad scientist," Jeff Hollinger.

◇ **Ice**
◇ **1¼ ounces brandy**
◇ **1 ounce Heering cherry liqueur**
◇ **¾ ounce fresh lemon juice**
◇ **2 dashes of Fee Brothers cherry bitters**
◇ **1 brandied cherry, for garnish**

◇ Fill a cocktail shaker with ice. Add all of the remaining ingredients except the garnish and shake well. Strain into a chilled coupe and garnish with the brandied cherry.

Coupe from Leo Design; "Service No. 4" decanter from Neue Galerie.

CHERRY SLIDECAR

the reinvention
BONDAGE

In this intensified Sidecar, Raglin replaces the orange curaçao with pear and ginger liqueurs and uses two bonded (aged, 100-proof) spirits: Laird's apple brandy and Ritten-house rye whiskey, which Raglin says tastes of "pumpernickel spice."

◇ **Ice**
◇ **¾ ounce bonded rye whiskey**
◇ **¾ ounce Laird's bonded apple brandy**
◇ **½ ounce each of ginger and pear liqueur**
◇ **¾ ounce fresh lemon juice**
◇ **Dash of orange bitters**
◇ **1 lemon twist, for garnish**

◇ Fill a cocktail shaker with ice. Add all of the remaining ingredients except the garnish and shake well. Strain into a chilled coupe and garnish with the lemon twist.

the mocktail
STEVE MCQUEEN

"I know that apples and ginger go well together, but my wife makes a ginger-and-orange doughnut that is nothing short of exquisite, so I combined the three flavors for this mocktail," Raglin says. He makes it with a gastrique, a syrup of vinegar, sugar and, typ-ically, fruit. Like a real cocktail, it has a sugared rim. (Note: The bitters in the drink are alcohol-based. For a completely nonalcoholic cocktail, leave them out.)

◇ **1 orange wedge and sugar**
◇ **Ice**
◇ **3 ounces chilled apple cider**
◇ **1½ ounces fresh orange juice**
◇ **1 ounce Ginger Gastrique (below)**
◇ **3 dashes of Fee Brothers Old Fashion aromatic bitters (optional)**

◇ Moisten the outer rim of a chilled coupe with the orange wedge; coat with sugar. Fill a shaker with ice. Add the remaining ingredients; shake well. Strain into the coupe.

GINGER GASTRIQUE

◇ In a saucepan, bring 4 ounces apple cider vinegar, 2 ounces sherry vinegar, 2 ounces water and ½ cup minced fresh ginger to a boil. Stir in 1 cup sugar; simmer over low heat for 20 minutes. Fine-strain into a heatproof jar. Let cool; refrigerate for up to 2 weeks. Makes about 8 ounces.

SINGAPORE SLING

Julie Reiner · Lani Kai · New York City

the classic
SINGAPORE SLING

"The Singapore Sling is one of my favorite tropical cocktails," says Julie Reiner. Most drink histories credit the recipe to a bartender named Ngiam Tong Boon, who's said to have mixed the first Sling around 1915 at the Long Bar inside Singapore's Raffles Hotel.

Ice
1½ ounces gin, preferably Plymouth
 1 ounce Sling Business (below)
1½ ounces chilled pineapple juice
 ½ ounce fresh lime juice
Dash of Angostura bitters
 1 brandied cherry skewered on a pick
    with 1 pineapple wedge, for garnish

Fill a cocktail shaker with ice. Add all of the remaining ingredients except the garnish and shake well. Strain into a chilled, ice-filled coupe and garnish the drink with the skewered cherry and pineapple wedge.

SLING BUSINESS
In a jar, combine ¼ ounce each of Heering cherry liqueur, Bénédictine (brandy-based herbal liqueur), grenadine (preferably homemade, **P.19**) and Cointreau or other triple sec. Makes 1 ounce.

the twist
LANI KAI SLING

Reiner created this rum-based Sling specifically for Lani Kai, her rum-centric, "modern tropical" restaurant and lounge.

- Ice
- 1 ounce white rhum agricole
- 1 ounce aged white rum, preferably El Dorado 3-Year
- 1 ounce Sling Business (p. 153)
- 1½ ounces chilled pineapple juice
- ½ ounce fresh lime juice
- Dash of Angostura bitters
- 1 umbrella plus 1 cherry skewered on a pick with 1 pineapple wedge, for garnish (optional)

Fill a cocktail shaker with ice. Add all of the remaining ingredients except the garnishes and shake well. Strain into a chilled, ice-filled collins glass. Garnish with the umbrella, cherry and pineapple.

the reinvention
STIRRED SLING

For this boozy, deconstructed Singapore Sling, Reiner removed all the juice (but added a lime-twist garnish) and replaced the gin with two kinds of rum: spicy Zafra, from Panama, and Jamaican Appleton Estate Reserve, which has notes of berries and pineapple.

- 1 ounce aged rum, preferably Jamaican
- 1 ounce dark rum, preferably Zafra
- ½ teaspoon Bénédictine (brandy-based herbal liqueur)
- ½ teaspoon maraschino liqueur
- ½ teaspoon Grand Marnier
- 2 dashes of orange bitters
- 1 lime twist, for garnish

Fill a pint glass with ice. Add all of the remaining ingredients except the garnish and stir well. Strain into a chilled coupe and garnish with the lime twist.

"Patrician" beer glass by Lobmeyr
from Kneen & Co.

LANI KAI SLING

SOUTHSIDE

Daniel Shoemaker · Teardrop Cocktail Lounge · Portland, OR

Y the classic
SOUTHSIDE

Said to have been invented by Chicago gangsters in the 1920s, this tangy summer cocktail has become a country club staple.

◇ **10 mint leaves, plus 2 mint sprigs for garnish**
◇ **Ice**
◇ **2 ounces gin**
◇ **¾ ounce fresh lemon juice**
◇ **½ ounce Rich Simple Syrup (p. 19)**
◇ **¼ ounce fresh lime juice**

◇ In a cocktail shaker, muddle the mint leaves. Add ice and the gin, lemon juice, Rich Simple Syrup and lime juice and shake well. Fine-strain (**P.18**) into a chilled coupe. Smack (**P.18**) the mint sprigs over the drink, then add them to the glass as garnish.

the twist
IMPERIAL SOUTHSIDE FIZZ

To mix this sparkling Southside, Daniel Shoemaker likes to shake the uncarbonated ingredients together first, then add the Champagne and "roll" the drink, or pour it back and forth between two shakers several times, before straining it into a collins glass. Bartenders use this technique when a fizzy drink needs more than a stir but shaking would make it too foamy.

- 10 mint leaves, plus 2 mint sprigs for garnish
- Ice
- 2 ounces gin
- ¾ ounce fresh lemon juice
- ¼ ounce fresh lime juice
- ½ ounce Rich Simple Syrup (p. 19)
- 2 dashes of Angostura bitters
- 1½ ounces chilled brut Champagne

In a cocktail shaker, muddle the mint leaves. Add ice and the gin, citrus juices, Rich Simple Syrup and bitters; shake well. Add the Champagne, then fine-strain (**P.18**) into an iced-filled collins glass. Smack (**P.18**) the mint sprigs over the drink, then add as garnish. Serve with 2 straws.

the reinvention
THE OTHER SIDE OF SUMMER

Shoemaker mixes an herby, subtly savory melon soda into the classic Southside. The result is great on a hot day.

- 10 mint leaves, plus 2 mint sprigs for garnish
- Ice
- 2 ounces gin
- ¾ ounce fresh lemon juice
- ¼ ounce fresh lime juice
- 2 dashes of Angostura bitters
- 4 ounces Melon Soda (p. 158)

In a shaker, muddle the mint leaves. Add ice and the gin, citrus juices and bitters; shake well. Add the Melon Soda. Fine-strain (**P.18**) into an iced-filled collins glass. Smack (**P.18**) the mint sprigs over the drink, then add as garnish.

the mocktail
MELON SODA

MAKES 8 DRINKS

Shoemaker cleverly combines dill, cilantro and cantaloupe juice in a soda that echoes the botanical flavors of the Southside's gin and mint. The soda can be mixed into cocktails (see The Other Side of Summer on P.157), but it's fantastic all by itself.

1½ cups Demerara or other raw sugar

6 ounces water

2 tablespoons chopped dill fronds

2 tablespoons chopped cilantro

20 ounces fresh cantaloupe juice (from 1 medium cantaloupe, juiced and strained)

1. In a medium saucepan, stir the sugar with the water over low heat until dissolved. Add the dill and cilantro and simmer for 10 minutes. Remove from the heat and let steep for 20 more minutes.

2. Strain the herb-infused syrup into a bowl and stir in the cantaloupe juice. Pour into a soda siphon (see Note) and refrigerate until chilled, about 1 hour. Seal the canister, shake hard and charge according to the manufacturer's directions with 1 or 2 CO_2 chargers. Dispense the soda into 8 chilled pilsner glasses.

NOTE Soda siphons and CO_2 chargers are available at kitchenware shops and *surlatable.com*.

MELON SODA

TOM & JERRY

John Gertsen · Drink · Boston

the classic
TOM & JERRY

MAKES 4 DRINKS

"It may seem like a bit of a nuisance to make such a labor-intensive drink," says John Gertsen of this classic 19th-century eggnog. *"But at the end of a long shift there's nothing better than a nice, hot Tom & Jerry."*

8 ounces Tom & Jerry Batter (below)
4 ounces Cognac
4 ounces aged rum
8 ounces hot whole milk
Freshly grated nutmeg, for garnish

Pour the Tom & Jerry Batter into a large heatproof measuring cup. Gently fold in the Cognac and rum, then gently stir in the hot milk. Pour the drink into 4 small warmed mugs or heatproof glasses. Garnish with nutmeg.

TOM & JERRY BATTER

In a medium bowl, beat 3 large egg whites with ⅛ teaspoon cream of tartar until soft peaks form. In another bowl, beat 3 egg yolks with ½ ounce aged rum. Gradually beat in 1 cup superfine sugar, ⅛ teaspoon ground cinnamon, ⅛ teaspoon ground mace, ⅛ teaspoon ground allspice and a small pinch of ground cloves. Gently fold in the beaten egg whites. The batter can be refrigerated overnight. Makes about 20 ounces.

Bar glasses from Moser.

TOM & JERRY

the twist
FERNET & JERRY

When Gertsen learned that Italian immigrants sometimes mix an obscure Sicilian bitters with eggnog as a kind of tonic, he had to try it. He substituted widely available Fernet-Branca for the bitters. The result? "The rich flavor of the egg takes the edge off the Fernet-Branca and the heat makes it smell heavenly."

2 ounces Tom & Jerry Batter (p. 160)
1½ ounces Fernet-Branca (bitter Italian digestif)
½ ounce Cognac
2 ounces hot whole milk
Freshly grated nutmeg, for garnish

Spoon the Tom & Jerry Batter into a small warmed mug or heatproof glass. Gently fold in the Fernet-Branca and Cognac, then gently stir in the hot milk. Garnish the drink with freshly grated nutmeg.

the reinvention
JOSEPH & JAMES

Gertsen created this chilled take on the Tom & Jerry for the Boston launch party of Banks 5-Island Rum in late 2010. Banks is an unusual blend of 21 white rums from five different countries: Barbados, Guyana, Jamaica, Java and Trinidad.

Ice cubes, plus crushed ice
2 ounces white rum, preferably Banks 5-Island
1½ ounces Tom & Jerry Batter (p. 160)
1 ounce chilled whole milk
Freshly grated nutmeg, for garnish

Fill a cocktail shaker with ice cubes. Add the rum, Tom & Jerry Batter and milk and shake well. Strain into a chilled, crushed ice–filled double rocks glass and garnish with freshly grated nutmeg. Serve with 2 straws.

TOM COLLINS

Marcos Tello • Killer Shrimp • Marina del Rey, CA

the classic
TOM COLLINS

Cocktail historians credit this classic summer gin drink to John Collins, a waiter at Limmer's Old House in 1800s London. The "Tom" part came along when bartenders began making it with Old Tom gin, which is slightly sweet. Although the name stuck, London dry gin now forms the base of the modern Tom Collins.

◇ **Ice**

◇ **1½ ounces London dry gin**

◇ **¾ ounce fresh lemon juice**

◇ **¾ ounce Simple Syrup (p. 19)**

◇ **2 ounces chilled club soda**

◇ **1 lemon twist, for garnish**

◇ Fill a chilled collins glass with ice. Add the gin, lemon juice and Simple Syrup and stir well. Stir in the club soda and garnish with the lemon twist.

the twist
BOURBON BLACKBERRY COLLINS

"You can mix and match a multitude of spirits and fruits or herbs in this recipe," says Marcos Tello. In place of the blackberries and bourbon, try raspberries and vodka or cherries and rum.

◇ **4 blackberries**
◇ **Ice**
◇ **1½ ounces bourbon**
◇ **¾ ounce fresh lemon juice**
◇ **¾ ounce Simple Syrup (p. 19)**
◇ **2 ounces chilled club soda**

◇ In a cocktail shaker, muddle 3 blackberries. Add ice and the bourbon, lemon juice and Simple Syrup and shake well. Strain into a chilled, ice-filled collins glass. Stir in the club soda and garnish with the remaining blackberry.

"Apollo" glass and "Twist" shot glasses by Nouvel Studio; swizzle stick by Orbix Hot Glass.

BOURBON BLACKBERRY COLLINS

MEASURING FIZZY INGREDIENTS

You've seen it before: A bartender, deep in conversation, adds spirits to a glass, then fills it the rest of the way with club soda, straight from the soda gun. Unfortunately, this method is wrong. Whether it's a simple spirit-and-soda drink or a slightly more involved variation like a Tom Collins (a mix of gin, lemon juice, simple syrup and club soda), the cocktail will suffer if the carbonated liquid is carelessly added to the glass. Doing so usually throws the drink out of balance or waters it down too much. It may seem fussy, but using a jigger to measure both the core ingredients and the carbonated ones will help ensure that you make the perfect cocktail every time.

the reinvention
BLACK TEA COLLINS

Tello calls this variation "a delicious sort of adult Arnold Palmer" (half iced tea and half lemonade). He suggests experimenting with the tea-spirit combination, perhaps trying a chai with Cognac or Thai tea with rum.

◇ **Ice**
◇ **1½ ounces Black Tea Vodka (below)**
◇ **¾ ounce fresh lemon juice**
◇ **¾ ounce Simple Syrup (p. 19)**
◇ **Dash of Angostura bitters**
◇ **2 ounces chilled club soda**
◇ **1 lemon twist, for garnish**

◇ Fill a chilled collins glass with ice. Add the Black Tea Vodka, lemon juice, Simple Syrup and bitters and stir well. Stir in the club soda and garnish with the lemon twist.

BLACK TEA VODKA

◇ In a jar, cover 1 tablespoon black tea leaves with 8 ounces vodka. Let steep for 20 minutes. Pour the infused vodka through a fine strainer into a clean jar and store at room temperature for up to 1 month. Makes 8 ounces.

the mocktail
SPARKLING BLACKBERRY SPRITZER

If you don't have blackberries or rosemary on hand, simply make this drink without them and garnish with a lemon twist. "It's the most delicious sparkling lemonade you'll ever have," says Tello.

◇ **5 blackberries and 2 rosemary sprigs**
◇ **Ice**
◇ **1 ounce fresh lemon juice**
◇ **1 ounce Simple Syrup (p. 19)**
◇ **4 ounces chilled club soda**

◇ In a chilled collins glass, muddle 3 blackberries with 1 rosemary sprig. Add ice and the lemon juice and Simple Syrup and stir well. Stir in the club soda and garnish with the remaining blackberries and rosemary sprig.

VESPER

Miles Macquarrie · Leon's Full Service · Decatur, GA

the classic
VESPER

James Bond created the Vesper in Ian Fleming's 1953 novel, Casino Royale. Bond instructs the bartender to shake the cocktail (of course), but Miles Macquarrie likes to stir his Vespers. This keeps the drink silky rather than frothy.

Ice, preferably cracked (p. 18)
1½ ounces London dry gin
¾ ounce vodka
½ ounce Lillet blanc
1 lemon twist, for garnish

Fill a pint glass with ice. Add the gin, vodka and Lillet blanc and stir well. Strain into a chilled coupe and garnish the drink with the lemon twist.

the twist
TRITON

This Vesper variation was inspired by the Seelbach Cocktail, a bourbon drink made with Cointreau, sparkling wine and a whopping 14 dashes of bitters. Macquarrie calls for a full quarter ounce of orange bitters here (he likes Regans'), which gives the cocktail a beautiful golden color.

Ice, preferably cracked (p. 18)
1 ounce London dry gin
¾ ounce Cocchi Americano or Lillet blanc
½ ounce Cointreau or other triple sec
¼ ounce orange bitters
2 ounces chilled sparkling wine, preferably Blanc de Blancs
1 lemon twist, for garnish

Fill a pint glass with ice. Add the gin, Cocchi Americano, Cointreau and bitters and stir well. Strain into a chilled coupe. Top with the sparkling wine and garnish the drink with the lemon twist.

VESPER

"Tulip" goblet by Paola C.

the reinvention
HONEY RYDER

Macquarrie loves finding alternatives to refined sugar for cocktails (see Trends on P.20). He sweetens this peppery drink with honey from local Georgia beehives.

Ice

1½ ounces gin, preferably Martin Miller's Westbourne Strength

½ ounce vodka, preferably potato-based vodka

½ ounce Lillet blanc

½ ounce fresh lemon juice

½ ounce honey syrup (2 teaspoons honey mixed with 1 teaspoon warm water)

¼ teaspoon Black Pepper Tincture (below)

1 lemon wheel, for garnish

Fill a cocktail shaker with ice. Add all of the remaining ingredients except the garnish and shake well. Strain into a chilled coupe and garnish with the lemon wheel.

BLACK PEPPER TINCTURE

In a jar, cover 1 tablespoon whole black peppercorns with 2 ounces overproof vodka. Let stand at room temperature for 1 week. Pour the tincture through a fine strainer into a clean jar. Store at room temperature for up to 1 month. Makes 2 ounces.

WHITE RUSSIAN

Francis Schott · Catherine Lombardi · New Brunswick, NJ

the classic
WHITE RUSSIAN

Many recipes for this 1970s cocktail call for light cream, but Francis Schott thinks it makes "an insipid drink." He confesses: "The first time I ordered a White Russian I'd snuck into a Chaka Khan concert; I didn't know what else to order."

Ice
- 2 ounces vodka
- 1 ounce coffee liqueur
- 2 ounces chilled heavy cream

Fill a cocktail shaker with ice. Add the vodka, coffee liqueur and heavy cream and shake well. Strain the drink into a chilled, ice-filled rocks glass.

the twist
CAFFÈ SALVATORE

Averna—the famous citrusy amaro from Sicily created by Salvatore Averna—gives this drink a bit of the bitterness of coffee. Horchata, a steeped drink that Schott cooks up with rice, almonds and sugar, makes the cocktail creamy.

Ice
- 2½ ounces Averna amaro
- ½ ounce vodka
- 2 ounces chilled horchata (see Note)

Fill a cocktail shaker with ice. Add the amaro, vodka and horchata and shake well. Strain the drink into a chilled, ice-filled rocks glass.

NOTE Horchata is sold at Latin markets, natural-food stores and some supermarkets.

the reinvention

■ BLACK BART

Root is a relatively new liqueur from a Philadelphia company called Art in the Age (artintheage.com). Distilled from sugarcane, it's flavored with birch bark, smoked black tea, citrus peels, cloves and other spices. Schott combines it with a cinnamon-infused simple syrup to create a replacement for coffee liqueur in the original White Russian. The result tastes like a spiked root beer float.

Ice

  2 ounces Root liqueur

  ¾ ounce white rum, preferably Banks 5-Island

  1 ounce chilled heavy cream

  ½ ounce Cinnamon Syrup (below)

  1 cinnamon stick and a pinch of ground cinnamon,
     for garnish

Fill a cocktail shaker with ice. Add all of the remaining ingredients except the garnishes and shake well. Fine-strain (P.18) into a chilled rocks glass and garnish with the cinnamon stick and ground cinnamon.

CINNAMON SYRUP

In a small saucepan, combine ½ cup Demerara or other raw sugar with 2 ounces water and ½ smashed cinnamon stick. Simmer over moderate heat for 10 minutes. Let cool, then strain the syrup into a jar and refrigerate for up to 2 weeks. Makes about 4 ounces.

BLACK BART

FLUKE CEVICHE **P.185**

WHITE SANGRIA **P.142**

PARTY FOOD

SCALLOP CEVICHE **P.184**

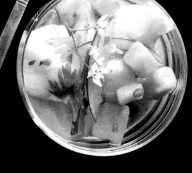

*"Squaresville" coaster set by Wolfum;
rocks and sake glasses by Deborah
Ehrlich from E.R. Butler & Co.*

bar nuts
SPICY MIXED NUTS
WITH ROSEMARY & CRANBERRIES
TOTAL: 20 MIN PLUS COOLING • MAKES 7 CUPS

At Drink, chef Colin Lynch adds a hit of cayenne to this snack for a little spice. He uses a mix of nuts; if you opt for just one kind, walnuts hold the seasonings especially well.

2 cups raw cashews

2 cups raw walnuts

2 cups raw almonds

2 tablespoons grapeseed oil

2 tablespoons finely chopped rosemary

1 tablespoon dark brown sugar

2 teaspoons kosher salt

¾ teaspoon cayenne pepper

1 cup dried cranberries

Preheat the oven to 350°. In a large bowl, toss the cashews, walnuts and almonds with the oil, rosemary, brown sugar, salt and cayenne. Spread on a rimmed baking sheet and bake for about 15 minutes, stirring halfway through baking, until golden. Let the nuts cool completely, then mix with the cranberries and serve.

DRINK
348 Congress St.
Boston • 617.695.1806
drinkfortpoint.com

bar nuts
CANDIED BACON CASHEWS
TOTAL: 20 MIN PLUS COOLING • MAKES ABOUT 5 CUPS

To make these cashews extra-indulgent, Lynch stirs in crispy bits of bacon and a little rendered bacon fat, too.

¼ pound slab bacon, cut into ¼-inch dice
½ cup sugar
4 cups raw cashews (1¼ pounds)
1 tablespoon unsalted butter
Smoked sea salt (see Note)

1. In a small skillet, cook the bacon over moderate heat until browned, about 7 minutes. Using a slotted spoon, transfer the bacon to a paper towel–lined plate. Measure out 1 tablespoon of the rendered bacon fat and reserve.
2. In a medium saucepan, combine the sugar with ½ cup of water and bring to a boil. Add the cashews and cook over high heat, stirring constantly, until golden, about 8 minutes. Stir in the butter and the reserved 1 tablespoon of bacon fat and cook over low heat, stirring, for 2 minutes. Stir in the diced bacon and season with smoked salt. Let cool completely, then serve.
NOTE Smoked sea salt is available at specialty food stores and from *surlatable.com.*

crostini

WILD MUSHROOM CROSTINI

TOTAL: 25 MIN • 8 SERVINGS

Southern cooking is often very meat-focused, but chef Ford Fry likes to emphasize vegetables. For these crostini, he tops creamy ricotta with a mix of garlicky mushrooms and a handful of herbs.

1 tablespoon unsalted butter
Extra-virgin olive oil
½ pound shiitake mushrooms, stems discarded and caps sliced ¼ inch thick
½ pound oyster mushrooms, sliced ½ inch thick
1 shallot, thinly sliced
2 garlic cloves, thinly sliced
¼ cup dry white wine
2 tablespoons fresh lemon juice
1 teaspoon finely chopped thyme
1 tablespoon finely chopped parsley, plus more for garnish
Kosher salt and freshly ground pepper
Four ½-inch-thick slices of rustic sourdough bread
½ pound fresh ricotta cheese (1 cup)
¼ cup each of tarragon leaves and snipped chives

1. In a large skillet, melt the butter in 1 tablespoon of olive oil. Add the shiitake and cook over moderately high heat, stirring, until browned, 4 minutes. Add the oyster mushrooms and cook until softened and lightly browned, 4 minutes. Add the shallot and garlic and cook until fragrant, 2 minutes. Stir in the wine, lemon juice, thyme and the 1 tablespoon of parsley. Season with salt and pepper.

2. Light a grill or preheat a grill pan. Brush the bread with olive oil and grill until toasted and charred in spots, about 1 minute per side.

3. Spread each toast slice with ¼ cup of the ricotta. Spoon the mushrooms on top and and sprinkle with the tarragon, chives and additional parsley. Cut the crostini in half, drizzle with olive oil and serve.

NO. 246
129 E. Ponce de Leon Ave.
Decatur, GA
678.399.8246
no246.com

WILD MUSHROOM CROSTINI

crostini

CHOPPED CHICKEN LIVER CROSTINI

ACTIVE: 30 MIN; TOTAL: 50 MIN • 6 TO 8 SERVINGS

The best chopped liver includes hard-cooked eggs. Fry firmly believes this: He adds a generous amount of chopped eggs, as well as a few piquant kalamata olives to his crostini topping.

Extra-virgin olive oil

½ pound chicken livers, trimmed

Kosher salt and freshly ground pepper

3 shallots, finely chopped

2 garlic cloves, thinly sliced

2 tablespoons chopped pitted kalamata olives

¼ cup dry white wine

Eighteen ⅓-inch-thick slices of baguette

2 tablespoons mayonnaise

2 teaspoons Dijon mustard

2 large hard-cooked eggs, coarsely chopped

⅓ cup chopped parsley, plus more for garnish

1. In a large cast-iron skillet, heat 2 tablespoons of olive oil. Season the livers with salt and pepper and cook over high heat until browned on one side, 4 minutes. Turn the livers and add the shallots, garlic and olives. Cook over moderately high heat, stirring occasionally, until the livers are barely pink inside, 4 minutes longer. Add the wine and cook over moderate heat until reduced by half, 2 minutes. Scrape into a food processor and let cool.

2. Preheat the oven to 350°. Arrange the baguette slices on a baking sheet and brush with olive oil. Bake for about 10 minutes, until golden.

3. Pulse the livers until coarsely chopped. Transfer to a bowl and mix in the mayonnaise and mustard. Fold in the eggs and the ⅓ cup of parsley; season with salt and pepper. Top the toasts with the chopped liver mixture, garnish with additional parsley and serve.

NO. 246

129 E. Ponce de Leon Ave.
Decatur, GA
678.399.8246
no246.com

chips
NACHOS
WITH PINTO BEANS & JACK CHEESE
TOTAL: 1 HR • 6 TO 8 SERVINGS

Be sure to use sturdy tortilla chips to support the mountain of toppings on chef Traci Des Jardins' nachos. She likes to make her own smoky-flavored salsa here; you can use a good store-bought version instead. These nachos are best served straight from the oven.

1 **pound tomatoes**
1 **white onion, halved lengthwise**
3 **garlic cloves**
2 **chipotles in adobo sauce, stemmed**
Kosher salt and freshly ground pepper
3 **poblano chiles**
One 1-pound bag tortilla chips
1 **pound Monterey Jack cheese, shredded**
One 15-ounce can pinto beans, rinsed and drained
Mexican *crema* or sour cream, guacamole, chopped cilantro and minced white onion, for serving

1. To make the salsa, light a grill or preheat a grill pan. Grill the tomatoes, halved onion and garlic over moderately high heat, turning, until charred in spots, about 10 minutes. In a saucepan, simmer the tomatoes, onion, garlic and chipotles with 1½ cups of water over moderate heat until the onion is softened and the tomatoes burst, about 30 minutes. Transfer to a blender and puree until smooth. Season the salsa with salt and pepper.
2. Roast the poblanos over a gas flame, turning, until charred. Transfer to a bowl, cover with plastic and let steam for 15 minutes. Peel, seed and stem the chiles, then dice.
3. Preheat the oven to 425°. Layer half of the chips on a foil-lined rimmed baking sheet. Scatter half of the cheese, beans and diced poblanos over the chips. Repeat the layering with the remaining chips, cheese, beans and poblanos. Drizzle half of the salsa on top and bake for about 10 minutes, until the cheese is melted. Drizzle *crema* over the nachos, top with guacamole and the remaining salsa, then sprinkle with cilantro and minced onion. Serve.

PUBLIC HOUSE
24 Willie Mays Plaza
San Francisco
415.644.0240
publichousesf.com

chips
CHIPS IN SALSA
ACTIVE: 30 MIN; TOTAL: 1 HR • 6 SERVINGS

In this best possible version of flavored tortilla chips, Des Jardins tosses the just-fried chips with homemade salsa, then sprinkles them with a little Mexican Cotija cheese.

½ **pound plum tomatoes**
½ **pound tomatillos, husked and rinsed**
 1 **medium white onion—half sliced crosswise ½ inch thick, the rest finely chopped for garnish**
 1 **tablespoon vegetable oil, plus more for frying**
 6 **dried árbol chiles**
 2 **garlic cloves, halved**
Kosher salt
12 **corn tortillas, each cut into 6 wedges, or one 1-pound bag sturdy, restaurant-style tortilla chips**
¼ **pound Cotija cheese, shredded**
½ **cup chopped cilantro**

1. To make the salsa, light a grill or preheat a grill pan. Grill the tomatoes, tomatillos and onion slices over moderately high heat, turning, until charred in spots, 10 minutes.
2. In a medium saucepan, heat the 1 tablespoon of oil. Add the árbol chiles and garlic and cook over moderately low heat until lightly browned, about 2 minutes. Add the grilled tomatoes, tomatillos and onion and 1½ cups of water. Simmer over moderately low heat until the onion is softened, about 30 minutes. Transfer to a blender and puree until smooth. Strain the salsa through a medium-mesh strainer; season with salt.
3. In a large saucepan, heat 2 inches of oil to 375°. Working in batches, fry the tortillas, turning occasionally, until golden and crisp. Using a slotted spoon, transfer the chips to a paper towel–lined plate to drain.
4. In a large bowl, toss the warm chips with half of the salsa. Transfer the chips in salsa to a platter and top with the cheese, cilantro and finely chopped onion. Serve right away, passing the remaining salsa at the table.

PUBLIC HOUSE
24 Willie Mays Plaza
San Francisco
415.644.0240
publichousesf.com

CHIPS IN SALSA

ceviche

SCALLOP CEVICHE
WITH SWEET POTATO

TOTAL: 20 MIN PLUS 1 HR MARINATING

6 TO 8 SERVINGS

Cevicherias, which are popular throughout Peru, are now appearing in the US. That's due at least in part to renowned Peruvian chef Gastón Acuria, who's opened branches of his Lima restaurant La Mar in San Francisco and Manhattan. In New York City, La Mar chef Victoriano López makes this recipe with aji limo paste, a Peruvian ceviche staple made from tiny ají chiles.

¼ cup fresh lime juice

¼ cup bottled clam juice or fish stock

2 tablespoons *ají limo* paste (see Note)

1 garlic clove

1 celery rib, chopped

½ cup thinly sliced red onion

½ cup chopped cilantro

1 large habanero chile, seeded and minced

Salt

1 pound large sea scallops, cut into ½-inch dice

½ sweet potato (4 ounces), peeled and cut into ½-inch dice

1. In a blender, combine the lime juice, clam juice, *ají limo* paste, garlic and celery with half each of the onion, cilantro and habanero. Blend until smooth. Strain the marinade through a fine strainer. Season with salt.

2. Spread the scallops in a single layer in a shallow glass or ceramic dish. Pour the marinade over the scallops. Cover and refrigerate until the scallops start to turn white, at least 1 hour and up to 4 hours.

3. Meanwhile, in a medium pot of boiling salted water, cook the sweet potato until tender, about 4 minutes. Transfer to a plate and sprinkle with salt. Let cool completely.

4. Stir the remaining onion, cilantro and habanero into the marinated scallops and season with salt. Spoon the ceviche into Chinese soup spoons or small bowls, top with the diced sweet potato and serve.

NOTE *Ají limo* paste is available at specialty food shops and *spanishtable.com*.

LA MAR CEBICHERIA

PERUANA

11 Madison Ave.

New York City

212.612.3388

lamarcebicheria.com

ceviche
FLUKE CEVICHE
WITH PERUVIAN CORN

TOTAL: 20 MIN PLUS 1 HR MARINATING
6 TO 8 SERVINGS

Peruvian corn has been cultivated for at least 3,000 years. An especially starchy variety, the corn is a little hard to find in the US but well worth seeking out for this recipe—it beautifully balances the sharp, acidic ceviche marinade.

½ cup fresh lime juice
½ cup bottled clam juice or fish stock
2 garlic cloves
1 large habanero chile, seeded and minced
½ cup thinly sliced red onion
¼ cup chopped cilantro
Salt
1½ pounds skinless fluke fillet, cut into
    ½-inch dice
Cooked Peruvian corn kernels (see Note),
    for garnish (optional)

1. In a blender, combine the lime juice, clam juice and garlic with half each of the habanero and onion and 1 tablespoon of the cilantro. Blend until smooth. Strain the marinade through a fine strainer; season with salt.

2. Spread the fluke in a single layer in a shallow glass or ceramic dish. Pour the marinade over the fluke. Cover and refrigerate until the fluke starts to turn white, at least 1 hour and up to 4 hours.

3. Stir the remaining habanero, onion and cilantro into the fluke and season with salt. Spoon the ceviche into Chinese soup spoons or small bowls and garnish with Peruvian corn kernels.

NOTE Peruvian corn is sold frozen on the cob at Latin markets and in the ethnic section of many supermarkets. Dried kernels are available at *tienda.com*.

french fries
PIMENTO CHEESE FRIES
ACTIVE: 30 MIN; TOTAL: 1 HR • 4 SERVINGS

To take his french fries over the top, chef Jonathon Sawyer broils them with a tequila-spiked pimento cheese topping. It's wonderfully decadent melted into the fries and also excellent as a dip.

¾ **pound aged white cheddar cheese, shredded**
¼ **cup blanco tequila**
2 **Fresno chiles**
1 **tablespoon butter**
1 **onion, finely diced**
¼ **cup mayonnaise**
2 **tablespoons chopped jarred pimientos**
1 **teaspoon paprika**
¼ **teaspoon cayenne pepper**
Smoked sea salt
Two 15-ounce packages frozen french fries or
 1 recipe unseasoned Pommes Frites (p. 188)

1. In a bowl, combine the cheese and tequila; refrigerate until the tequila is absorbed, about 30 minutes.
2. Roast the chiles directly over a gas flame or under a preheated broiler, turning, until charred all over. Peel, seed and stem the chiles, then cut into ¼-inch dice.
3. In a medium skillet, melt the butter. Add the onion and cook over moderately low heat until softened, about 7 minutes. Scrape the onion into the infused cheese. Add the mayonnaise, pimientos, paprika, cayenne and chiles. Season the pimento cheese with smoked sea salt.
4. Preheat the oven to 425°. Spread the french fries on a rimmed baking sheet in a single layer. Bake for 20 to 25 minutes, until browned and crisp. Remove the fries from the oven and preheat the broiler. Spoon the pimento cheese over the fries and broil 4 to 6 inches from the heat for 3 to 5 minutes, until the cheese is melted and browned in spots. Serve right away.

**THE GREENHOUSE
TAVERN**
2038 E. Fourth St.
Cleveland • 216.443.0511
thegreenhousetavern.com

Ceramic pan by 4th-Market from Baum-Kuchen; "Linking Trellis" lacquered tray by DwellStudio.

POMMES FRITES P.188

PIMENTO CHEESE FRIES

POMMES FRITES
french fries
ACTIVE: 30 MIN; TOTAL: 1 HR 15 MIN • 4 SERVINGS

Sawyer is something of a french fry expert: There are never fewer than three kinds on the menu at the Greenhouse Tavern. This version, tossed with chopped garlic and herbs, is his most straightforward. At the restaurant, he serves the fries with garlicky aioli.

2 pounds baking potatoes, peeled and cut into ¼-inch-thick sticks
Vegetable oil, for frying
4 garlic cloves, crushed
1 tablespoon finely chopped rosemary
Salt
Dijon mustard, for serving

1. In a medium bowl, cover the potato sticks with water and let stand for 15 minutes. Drain, then rinse the potatoes and pat thoroughly dry.

2. In a large saucepan, heat 2 inches of oil to 275°. Line a baking sheet with paper towels. Working in batches, fry the potatoes until almost tender and slightly translucent, about 5 minutes. Transfer the potatoes to the paper towels to drain. Refrigerate for 30 minutes.

3. Reheat the oil to 350°. In a mortar, pound the garlic with the rosemary and a pinch of salt until a paste forms. Fry the potatoes in batches until golden and crisp, about 5 minutes. Using a slotted spoon, transfer the fries to a baking sheet and immediately season with salt. Toss with the garlic-rosemary paste and serve the fries right away, with Dijon mustard alongside.

THE GREENHOUSE TAVERN
2038 E. Fourth St.
Cleveland • 216.443.0511
thegreenhousetavern.com

fried squid
THAI-STYLE FRIED SQUID
WITH CHILE-LIME MAYONNAISE

TOTAL: 25 MIN • 4 SERVINGS

This dish is a longtime favorite at star chef Jean-Georges Vongerichten's Mercer Kitchen. He serves the crispy squid with a bright chile-and-lime-spiked mayonnaise.

1 cup mayonnaise
1 teaspoon finely grated lemon zest, plus 1 tablespoon fresh lemon juice
1 teaspoon finely grated lime zest, plus 1 tablespoon fresh lime juice
1 Thai chile, minced
Sea salt and freshly ground pepper
Vegetable oil, for frying
2 large egg whites
Cornstarch, for dusting
1 pound cleaned small squid, bodies cut crosswise into ½-inch rings, tentacles halved

1. In a small bowl, whisk the mayonnaise with the lemon and lime zests and juices and the Thai chile. Season the mayonnaise with salt and pepper.

2. In a large saucepan, heat 1 inch of vegetable oil to 350°. Set a rack over a rimmed baking sheet. In a shallow bowl, beat the egg whites. Spread cornstarch in another shallow bowl. Working in four batches, dip the squid in the egg whites; press out any excess egg. Dredge the squid in the cornstarch and shake off any excess. Fry the squid in the hot vegetable oil until golden and crisp, about 2 minutes. Using a slotted spoon, transfer the squid to the rack. Season lightly with salt and pepper. Transfer the fried squid to a platter and serve immediately, with the chile-lime mayonnaise.

MERCER KITCHEN
99 Prince St.
New York City
212.966.5454
jean-georges.com

fried squid
PRETZEL-CRUSTED SQUID
WITH MUSTARD DIPPING SAUCE

TOTAL: 25 MIN • 4 SERVINGS

Crushed hard pretzels make a great crust for fried squid. Because mustard is a natural with pretzels, Vongerichten uses it in his creamy, tangy dipping sauce.

½ cup mayonnaise
¼ cup Dijon mustard
1 tablespoon whole-grain mustard
1 tablespoon fresh lemon juice
Kosher salt and freshly ground pepper
8 ounces hard pretzels, crushed
2 large egg whites
Vegetable oil, for frying
1 pound cleaned small squid,
    bodies cut crosswise into ½-inch rings,
    tentacles halved

1. In a small bowl, whisk the mayonnaise with both mustards and the lemon juice; season with salt and pepper.
2. In a food processor or blender, pulse the pretzels until they resemble cornmeal. Transfer to a shallow bowl. In another shallow bowl, beat the egg whites until frothy.
3. In a large saucepan, heat 1 inch of vegetable oil to 350°. Set a rack over a rimmed baking sheet. Working in four batches, dip the squid in the egg; press out any excess egg. Dredge the squid in the pretzel crumbs and shake off any excess. Fry the squid in the hot oil until golden and crisp, about 2 minutes. Using a slotted spoon, transfer the squid to the rack. Season lightly with salt and pepper. Transfer the squid to a platter and serve right away, with the mustard dipping sauce.

ABC KITCHEN
35 E. 18th St.
New York City
212.475.5829
abckitchennyc.com

tacos
BIG STAR TACOS
WITH CHILES, CHORIZO & MONTEREY JACK CHEESE
TOTAL: 1 HR • 4 SERVINGS

"It's a marriage of Mexico and America, tacos and bourbon," says chef Justin Large about Big Star, the convivial spot co-owned by star chef Paul Kahan. Large's rich, hearty tacos get great heat from two kinds of roasted chiles, plus fresh chorizo.

- 4 poblano chiles and 4 Anaheim chiles
- 1 tablespoon extra-virgin olive oil
- ½ pound fresh Mexican chorizo, casings discarded
- 2 yellow onions, halved lengthwise and thinly sliced crosswise
- 4 garlic cloves, thinly sliced
- 4 bay leaves
- 1 teaspoon dried oregano
- ⅔ cup crème fraîche
- 4 ounces Monterey Jack cheese, shredded (1 cup)

Kosher salt
- 12 warm corn tortillas

Salsa, for serving

1. Roast the poblano and Anaheim chiles directly over a gas flame or under a preheated broiler, turning, until charred all over. Transfer the chiles to a bowl, cover with plastic wrap and let steam for 15 minutes. Peel, seed and stem the chiles, then cut into ¼-inch strips.

2. In a skillet, heat the oil. Add the chorizo and cook over moderate heat until browned and cooked through, 5 minutes. Using a slotted spoon, transfer the chorizo to a plate. Add the onions to the skillet and cook over moderate heat until browned, 10 minutes. Add the garlic, bay leaves and oregano and cook until the onions are softened, 5 minutes longer. Discard the bay leaves.

3. Add the chiles, chorizo, crème fraîche and cheese to the skillet. Cook over moderate heat, stirring, until the cheese is melted, 5 minutes. Season with salt. Spoon the filling into the warm tortillas and serve with salsa.

BIG STAR
1531 N. Damen Ave.
Chicago • 773.235.4039
bigstarchicago.com

tacos

CHICKEN & POBLANO TACOS WITH CREMA

TOTAL: 45 MIN • 4 SERVINGS

This is a variation on the chorizo tacos that Large makes at Big Star. You can replace the chicken strips with chorizo; for a vegetarian taco, Large recommends subbing in crumbled spiced tofu.

5 poblano chiles
4 boneless chicken thighs with skin (1 pound),
   pounded ½ inch thick
Extra-virgin olive oil, for brushing
Kosher salt and freshly ground pepper
½ cup chopped cilantro
12 warm corn tortillas
Mexican *crema* or sour cream, shredded romaine
   lettuce, chopped white onion and lime wedges,
   for serving

1. Roast the poblanos directly over a gas flame or under a preheated broiler, turning, until charred all over. Transfer the chiles to a bowl, cover with plastic wrap and let steam for 15 minutes. Peel, seed and stem the chiles, then cut them into ¼-inch strips.

2. Light a grill or preheat a grill pan. Brush the chicken all over with oil and season with salt and pepper. Grill over moderately high heat, turning once, until the skin is crisp and browned, about 8 minutes. Transfer the chicken to a carving board and cut into ½-inch strips.

3. In a medium bowl, toss the poblano strips with the chicken and cilantro and season with salt and pepper. Serve the chicken-poblano filling in the warm tortillas with the *crema*, lettuce, onion and lime wedges.

BIG STAR
1531 N. Damen Ave.
Chicago • 773.235.4039
bigstarchicago.com

CHICKEN & POBLANO TACOS WITH CREMA

"Labyrinth" lacquered tray by DwellStudio.

grilled cheese
WHITE CHEDDAR MELTS
WITH MOSTARDA & ARUGULA
TOTAL: 45 MIN • MAKES 4 SANDWICHES

Top Chef Season 6 winner Michael Voltaggio creates incredible sandwiches at his tiny new L.A. restaurant Ink Sack. Instead of the usual mustard, he flavors this grilled cheese with mostarda— a tangy, fruity condiment made with a mix of apple, dried apricots, orange juice, mustard and spices.

Extra-virgin olive oil
½ Granny Smith apple—peeled, cored and diced
½ cup dried apricots, cut into ¼-inch dice
¼ cup brown sugar
1 tablespoon apple cider vinegar
One 1-inch cinnamon stick
½ teaspoon finely grated orange zest
¼ cup fresh orange juice
½ cup whole-grain mustard
Kosher salt and freshly ground pepper
Eight ½-inch-thick slices of rustic sourdough bread
¾ pound sharp white cheddar, cut into 12 slices
2 cups baby arugula

1. In a medium saucepan, heat 2 teaspoons of olive oil. Add the apple and apricots and cook over moderate heat, stirring, until just softened, 5 minutes. Add the sugar, vinegar, cinnamon stick and orange zest and juice. Cook over moderately low heat, stirring occasionally, until thickened, 8 minutes. Remove from the heat; discard the cinnamon stick. Stir in the mustard and season with salt and pepper. Let the *mostarda* cool completely.

2. Preheat a griddle over moderately low heat. Brush one side of each bread slice with olive oil. On the other side of 4 bread slices, spread with the *mostarda* (¼ cup each), then top each with 3 slices of cheddar. Close the sandwiches, set them on the hot griddle and top with a large baking sheet weighted down with cans. Cook over moderately low heat until toasted, 3 minutes per side. Open the sandwiches and tuck ½ cup of the arugula into each. Close the sandwiches, cut in half and serve hot.

INK SACK
8360 Melrose Ave.
Los Angeles
323.655.7225
mvink.com

grilled cheese
AGED CHEDDAR BITES
WITH SPICED KETCHUP
TOTAL: 1 HR • MAKES 16 CHEDDAR BITES

Voltaggio stuffs chunks of homemade onion-studded brioche with cheese and a complex curry ketchup, then deep-fries them. This simplified recipe calls for store-bought pizza dough and an easy version of the ketchup for dipping.

- 1 tablespoon extra-virgin olive oil
- 1 small onion, minced
- ½ cup ketchup
- 1 teaspoon finely grated fresh ginger
- 1 teaspoon Madras curry powder
- 1 teaspoon soy sauce
- 1 small garlic clove, finely grated

Kosher salt
- ½ pound extra-sharp cheddar cheese, shredded
- ½ pound pizza dough, divided into 16 balls

Vegetable oil, for frying

1. In a small skillet, heat 2 teaspoons of the olive oil. Add the onion and cook over moderately low heat until caramelized, 15 minutes. Scrape into a bowl and let cool.

2. In a small bowl, whisk the ketchup with the ginger, curry powder, soy sauce, garlic and the remaining 1 teaspoon of oil; season with salt. Scrape half of the spiced ketchup into the bowl with the onion; stir in the cheese.

3. On a lightly floured work surface, roll out the dough balls into 3-inch rounds. Spoon 1 tablespoon of the cheese filling onto the center of each round. Bring up the dough around the filling and press to seal in the cheese.

4. In a large saucepan, heat 1 inch of oil to 325°. Fry the cheese bites in batches, turning occasionally, until golden and puffed, about 5 minutes. Using a slotted spoon, transfer the bites to a paper towel–lined plate to drain. Serve right away, with the remaining spiced ketchup for dipping.

charcuterie
CHARCUTERIE WITH HOMEMADE MUSTARD

TOTAL: 15 MIN • MAKES ABOUT 1¼ CUPS

Chef Erick Harcey cures all of his own charcuterie and serves it with this bold, slightly sweet mustard. He makes the mustard with his favorite local coffee, Dogwood espresso; indeed, he's such a coffee fan that he decided to become a barista-in-training at his new place, Victory 44 Coffee Bar and Provisions.

3 tablespoons black mustard seeds
½ cup Dijon mustard
¼ cup hot English mustard, such as Coleman's
2 tablespoons blackstrap molasses
2 tablespoons brewed espresso
2 tablespoons honey
2 tablespoons vegetable oil
2 teaspoons rice vinegar
1 teaspoon whiskey
Sea salt
Cured meats and pretzels, for serving

1. In a small skillet, toast the mustard seeds over moderate heat until they just start to pop, about 3 minutes.
2. In a blender, combine the toasted mustard seeds with both mustards and the molasses, espresso, honey, oil, vinegar and whiskey. Blend until smooth with some specks of seeds still visible. Season with salt. Scrape the mustard into a bowl and serve with cured meats and pretzels.

VICTORY 44
2203 44th Ave. North
Minneapolis
612.588.2228
victory-44.com

charcuterie

MORTADELLA & ROBIOLA PANINI
WITH HOMEMADE MUSTARD

TOTAL: 40 MIN • MAKES 4 PANINI

This panini makes excellent use of leftover charcuterie, like the porky mortadella suggested here, but you can also use country ham or prosciutto. Sometimes, when Harcey is craving an even more lavish sandwich, he'll add an extra layer of Robiola.

8   slices of seeded Jewish rye bread
Unsalted butter, softened, for brushing
½   cup homemade mustard (recipe opposite)
1   pound thinly sliced mortadella
½   pound Robiola Bosina cheese, cut into
     12 equal slices with the rind
1   cup lightly packed baby arugula
¼   cup pickled red onion slices or 12 pickled
     cocktail onions, thinly sliced

1. Preheat a panini press or a griddle. Brush one side of each bread slice with butter and arrange buttered side down on a work surface. Spread each bread slice with 1 tablespoon of the mustard. Layer the mortadella, Robiola, arugula and pickled onions on 4 of the bread slices and close the sandwiches.

2. Grill the panini over moderate heat until browned and crisp outside, about 3 minutes in a press or 3 minutes per side on a griddle. Cut the panini in half and serve.

fried chicken

BUTTERMILK FRIED CHICKEN
WITH MADRAS CURRY

TOTAL: 45 MIN PLUS OVERNIGHT MARINATING

4 SERVINGS

Paul Qui, the Top Chef star from Texas, adds a secret ingredient to the batter for his chicken: Madras curry powder.

- 2 cups buttermilk
- 6 garlic cloves, crushed
- 2 Thai chiles, chopped

One 1-inch piece of fresh ginger, crushed

Kosher salt

One 4-pound chicken, cut into 8 pieces

- 2 cups all-purpose flour
- 1 tablespoon Madras curry powder

Vegetable or canola oil, for frying

Thai sweet chile sauce, for serving

1. In a large bowl, combine the buttermilk, garlic, Thai chiles, ginger and 1 teaspoon of salt. Add the chicken and turn to coat. Cover and refrigerate overnight.

2. Set a rack over a baking sheet. In a large, resealable plastic bag, mix the flour, curry powder and 1 tablespoon of salt and shake to blend. Remove the chicken from the buttermilk, letting the excess drip back into the bowl, then dredge the chicken in the flour mixture. Transfer the coated chicken to the rack.

3. In a large, deep skillet, heat 1 inch of oil to 350°. Set another rack over a rimmed baking sheet. Fry the chicken at 300°, turning once, until golden and an instant-read thermometer inserted in the thickest part of each piece registers 160°, 15 to 18 minutes. Transfer the fried chicken to the rack and let stand for 5 minutes before serving with the sweet chile sauce.

UCHIKO

4200 N. Lamar

Austin • 512.916.4808

uchiaustin.com/uchiko

PISCO SOUR P.125

BUTTERMILK FRIED CHICKEN

"String" glasses from Calvin Klein Home; vintage bowl from The End of History; "Tasaraita" napkin from Marimekko.

fried chicken
CHILE-MARINATED FRIED CHICKEN

TOTAL: 1 HR PLUS OVERNIGHT MARINATING

4 SERVINGS

In his outstanding Asian twist on Southern fried chicken, Qui uses chile sauce in both the marinade and the sweet, sticky sauce that's tossed with the chicken before serving.

¾ cup Thai sweet chile sauce

½ cup plus 2 tablespoons fish sauce

One 4-pound chicken, cut into 8 pieces

1 cup palm sugar or light brown sugar

¼ cup minced cilantro stems

1 tablespoon minced fresh lemongrass (tender inner core only)

1 tablespoon *sambal oelek* or other Asian hot chile sauce

1 cup cornstarch

Vegetable oil, for frying

1. In a bowl, whisk ¼ cup of the sweet chile sauce with ¼ cup of water and 2 tablespoons of the fish sauce. Add the chicken; turn to coat. Cover and refrigerate overnight.

2. In a small saucepan, combine the remaining ½ cup of fish sauce with the palm sugar, cilantro, lemongrass and *sambal oelek*. Simmer over moderate heat until reduced to ½ cup, about 8 minutes. Strain the sauce through a fine strainer into a bowl. Stir in the remaining ½ cup of sweet chile sauce; let cool.

3. Spread the cornstarch in a shallow bowl. Remove the chicken from the marinade, scraping the excess back into the bowl. Dredge the chicken in the cornstarch.

4. In a large, deep skillet, heat 1 inch of oil to 350°. Fry the chicken at 300°, turning once, until golden and an instant-read thermometer inserted in the thickest part of each piece registers 160°, 15 to 18 minutes. Transfer the fried chicken to the sauce and toss to coat. Arrange the chicken on a platter and serve right away.

UCHIKO

4200 N. Lamar

Austin · 512.916.4808

uchiaustin.com/uchiko

hot dogs
GRILLED PICKLED HOT DOGS
WITH MUSTARD RELISH

TOTAL: 40 MIN PLUS OVERNIGHT PICKLING

6 SERVINGS

Many people add pickled condiments to their hot dogs. Phillip Kirschen-Clark of New York City's Demi Monde, who developed this recipe as a Crif Dogs "guest chef," has other ideas: He pickles the hot dog itself, in an apple cider vinegar. Then he grills it and serves it with sauerkraut and creamy mustard relish.

1   cup apple cider vinegar
¼   cup sugar
2   tablespoons kosher salt
2   garlic cloves
2   bay leaves
6   hot dogs
½   cup mayonnaise
¼   cup finely chopped dill pickles
2   tablespoons whole-grain mustard
2   tablespoons Dijon mustard
1   teaspoon honey
6   hot dog buns, split and warmed
Sauerkraut, for serving

1. In a small saucepan, bring the vinegar, sugar, salt, garlic, bay leaves and 1 cup of water to a boil. Remove from the heat and let cool completely. Prick the hot dogs all over with a toothpick and set them in an 8-inch square glass or ceramic casserole. Pour the pickling brine over the hot dogs, cover and refrigerate overnight.

2. In a bowl, whisk the mayonnaise with the pickles, both mustards and the honey.

3. Light a grill or preheat a grill pan. Pat the hot dogs dry with paper towels. Grill over high heat until lightly charred and heated through, about 4 minutes. Tuck the hot dogs into the warmed buns, top with the mustard relish and sauerkraut and serve.

CRIF DOGS

113 Saint Marks Pl.
New York City
212.614.2728
crifdogs.com

hot dogs
FRIED BACON–WRAPPED HOT DOGS
WITH COCKTAIL SAUCE

TOTAL: 1 HR • 6 SERVINGS

Chef Nick Licata of Jack's Luxury Oyster Bar in Manhattan created this recipe for Crif Dogs. Inspired by the variety of sauces that accompany raw shellfish, he tops his decadent bacon-wrapped hot dogs with a home-made horseradish-spiked cocktail sauce and deli-cious anchovy butter.

One 15-ounce can diced tomatoes, drained

1½ tablespoons prepared horseradish

2 teaspoons Louisiana-style hot sauce

1 teaspoon Worcestershire sauce

1 tablespoon vegetable oil, plus more for frying

1 teaspoon finely grated lemon zest

2 teaspoons fresh lemon juice

Kosher salt and freshly ground pepper

1 stick unsalted butter, softened

3 tablespoons finely chopped parsley

1 tablespoon anchovy paste

1 teaspoon pimentón de la Vera

6 bacon slices, 6 hot dogs and 6 warm hot dog buns

Crispy potato sticks, for serving

1. In a food processor, combine the tomatoes, horseradish, hot sauce, Worcestershire sauce, the 1 tablespoon of oil, ½ teaspoon of the lemon zest and 1 teaspoon of the lemon juice. Puree until smooth; season with salt and pepper. Transfer the cocktail sauce to a bowl.

2. In a small bowl, blend the butter, parsley, anchovy paste, pimentón and the remaining lemon zest and lemon juice. Season with salt and pepper.

3. In a large skillet, heat ½ inch of oil. Wrap a bacon slice around each hot dog and secure with toothpicks. Fry the hot dogs over moderate heat, turning, until the bacon is crisp, 5 minutes. Transfer the hot dogs to paper towels to drain, then tuck into the buns. Top with the anchovy butter, cocktail sauce and potato sticks and serve.

CRIF DOGS
113 Saint Marks Pl.
New York City
212.614.2728
crifdogs.com

burgers
CHEDDAR & ONION SMASHED BURGERS

TOTAL: 30 MIN • MAKES 4 BURGERS

At Adam Fleischman's expanding Los Angeles chain, the secret to his burgers is "umami dust," a combination of bonito (dried tuna) flakes, dried kombu (seaweed) and shiitake mushrooms with a pronounced savory Asian flavor. It makes a juicy burger taste even more deeply meaty.

16   thin bread-and-butter pickle slices, patted dry
Four 4-inch potato buns, buttered and toasted
1¼   pounds ground beef chuck (30 percent fat)
Salt and freshly ground pepper
2   small onions, sliced paper-thin
4   ounces sharp cheddar cheese, sliced
Umami Dust, for sprinkling (optional, recipe below)

1. Heat a cast-iron griddle until very hot. Layer the pickle slices on the bottom buns.

2. Without overworking the ground meat, loosely form it into 4 balls and place them on the griddle. Cook over moderately high heat for 30 seconds. Using a sturdy, large spatula, flatten each ball into a 5-inch round patty. Season the patties with salt and pepper and cook for 2 minutes, until well seared. Press a handful of sliced onions onto each patty. Using the spatula, carefully flip each burger so the onions are on the bottom. Top with the cheese; cook for 2 minutes. Cover with an inverted roasting pan and cook just until the cheese is melted, 1 minute more. Transfer the burgers with the onions to the buns and sprinkle with Umami Dust. Top with the buns and serve right away.

UMAMI DUST

In a spice grinder, pulse 3 tablespoons bonito flakes, ½ ounce crumbled dried kombu and ½ ounce dried shiitake mushrooms into a powder. Keep in a sealed jar at room temperature for up to 2 months. Makes 2½ ounces.

UMAMI BURGER
850 S. La Brea Ave.
Los Angeles
323.931.3000
umamiburger.com

burgers
UMAMI BURGERS
WITH PORT & STILTON
TOTAL: 40 MIN • MAKES 4 BURGERS

Fleischman says the key to a great burger is to cook it on a griddle: "You get a more even sear, and the fat bastes the burger instead of dripping through the grate."

1 cup ruby port
2 pounds mixed ground beef brisket, skirt steak and sirloin steak (20 percent fat)
Salt and freshly ground pepper
½ cup Stilton cheese (3 ounces), softened
Umami Dust, for sprinkling (optional, recipe, p. 203)
4 brioche hamburger buns, buttered and toasted

1. In a small saucepan, cook the port over moderate heat until reduced to 2 tablespoons, about 15 minutes.
2. Heat a cast-iron griddle until very hot. Form the meat into four 4-by-1-inch patties without packing too tightly. Season generously with salt and pepper. Arrange the patties on the griddle, cover with a roasting pan and cook over moderately high heat for 4 minutes, until very crusty. Flip the patties and cook, covered, for 2 minutes longer; top with the Stilton and cook uncovered for 1 minute. Transfer the patties to a plate and sprinkle with the Umami Dust. Let rest for 2 minutes, then set on the buns. Drizzle with the reduced port, top with the buns and serve.

UMAMI BURGER
850 S. La Brea Ave.
Los Angeles
323.931.3000
umamiburger.com

MICHELADA GINGEMBRE P.108

UMAMI BURGER

"Gold Ribbons" glass by DwellStudio.

ribs

GRILLED SPARERIBS
WITH PEDRO XIMÉNEZ VINEGAR

TOTAL: 45 MIN PLUS 8 HR MARINATING

4 SERVINGS

Chef Seamus Mullen loves cooking his ribs on a grill, the Spanish way, which adds an extra layer of smokiness to the meat. At Tertulia, he uses ribs from Iberian pigs that eat only acorns. "The meat isn't cheap, but it's worth every peseta," says Mullen.

3 tablespoons extra-virgin olive oil

2 garlic cloves, minced

1 tablespoon minced thyme

1 tablespoon minced rosemary

1 rack of pork spareribs (2½ pounds)

Kosher salt and freshly ground pepper

1 cup Pedro Ximénez vinegar or sherry vinegar

1. In a small bowl, whisk the olive oil with the garlic, thyme and rosemary. Set the spareribs in a baking dish and season with salt and pepper. Rub the garlic mixture all over the ribs and cover with plastic wrap; refrigerate for at least 8 hours or overnight.

2. In a small saucepan, simmer the vinegar over moderately low heat until reduced to ¼ cup, about 8 minutes.

3. Light a grill or preheat the broiler. Grill the ribs over moderately high heat, turning occasionally, until lightly charred and cooked through, 15 to 20 minutes. Brush the ribs with some of the reduced vinegar and grill, turning, until nicely glazed, about 5 minutes longer. Cut the ribs between the bones, transfer to a platter and serve.

TERTULIA

359 Sixth Ave.
New York City
646.559.9909
tertulianyc.com

ribs
GRILLED LAMB RIBS
WITH GLAZED SHIITAKE MUSHROOMS
TOTAL: 45 MIN • 2 TO 4 SERVINGS

Lamb ribs have become more popular with chefs like Mullen who appreciate the flavor and value of this underused cut of meat. Since lamb ribs aren't very big, they're an ideal cocktail snack.

½ cup Pedro Ximénez vinegar or sherry vinegar

2 tablespoons unsalted butter

2 tablespoons extra-virgin olive oil, plus more for brushing

1 pound shiitake mushrooms, stems discarded and caps sliced

Kosher salt and freshly ground pepper

1 rack of lamb spareribs (about 1 pound), cut into individual ribs

1. In a small saucepan, simmer the vinegar over moderately low heat until reduced to ⅓ cup, about 5 minutes.

2. In a large skillet, melt the butter in the 2 tablespoons of olive oil. Add the mushrooms and cook over high heat, turning once, until golden, about 5 minutes. Add 3 tablespoons of the reduced vinegar and cook over low heat until the mushrooms are nicely glazed and tender, about 3 minutes. Season with salt and pepper.

3. Light a grill or preheat the broiler. Brush the ribs with olive oil and season with salt and pepper. Grill the ribs over moderate heat, turning occasionally, until lightly charred and cooked through, 15 to 20 minutes. Brush the ribs with the remaining vinegar and grill, turning, until nicely glazed, about 5 minutes. Transfer the ribs to a platter and serve the mushrooms alongside.

CURE IN NEW ORLEANS, P.213

TOP 100 AMERICAN BARS

F&W's editors compiled this definitive listing of the country's best bars, lounges and restaurants, many of them featured in this book.

EAST COAST

BOSTON

BRICK & MORTAR
This new lounge above Central Kitchen features drinks by cocktail expert Misty Kalkofen. *567 Massachusetts Ave.; 617.491.5599.*

DRINK P.160
Star chef Barbara Lynch's bar dispenses with menus; mixologist John Gertsen and his team custom-make drinks for each guest. *348 Congress St.; 617.695.1806.*

THE HAWTHORNE P.87
Jackson Cannon's new place is named for his favorite bar tool, the Hawthorne strainer. *500A Commonwealth Ave.; 617.532.9150.*

ISLAND CREEK OYSTER BAR
This shellfish destination serves drinks like the 1822 (gin and rhubarb-infused vermouth). *500 Commonwealth Ave.; 617.532.5300.*

NEW YORK CITY

THE BEAGLE
This cozy spot pairs food and spirits such as pickled mackerel with Aalborg aquavit. *162 Avenue A, Manhattan; 212.228.6900.*

CLOVER CLUB
Julie Reiner's stylish classic-cocktails venue is named for a pre-Prohibition men's club. *210 Smith St., Brooklyn; 718.855.7939.*

DEATH & CO. P.90
Joaquín Simó and his fellow bartenders have an encyclopedic knowledge of cocktails. *433 E. Sixth St., Manhattan; 212.388.0882.*

DRAM
A rotating team of acclaimed bartenders serves drinks on draft, barrel-aged cocktails and other innovations. *177 S. Fourth St., Brooklyn; 718.486.3726; drambar.com.*

DUTCH KILLS
Mixologist Richard Boccato's bar is modeled after an 1890s "gentlemen's tavern." *27-24 Jackson Ave., Long Island City; 718.383.2724; dutchkillsbar.com.*

ELEVEN MADISON PARK P.68
Leo Robitschek's inventive cocktails complement chef Daniel Humm's divine menu. *11 Madison Ave., Manhattan; 212.889.0905.*

EMPLOYEES ONLY P.38
This bartender-owned supper club was designed to be a haven for fellow mixologists. *510 Hudson St., Manhattan; 212.242.3021.*

MAISON PREMIERE
An 1800s-style oyster house, this intimate spot has NYC's largest selection of absinthes and absinthe cocktails. *298 Bedford Ave., Brooklyn; 347.335.0446.*

MAYAHUEL
Death & Co. alum Philip Ward co-owns this traditional mezcal and tequila bar. *304 E. Sixth St., Manhattan; 212.253.5888.*

NEW YORK CITY CONTINUED

MILK & HONEY
Sam Ross and Michael McIlroy are in charge of drinks at this tiny, reservations-only lounge. *134 Eldridge St., Manhattan; no phone; mlkhny.com.*

PDT P.61
Mixologist Jim Meehan, deputy editor of *F&W Cocktails 2012*, obsesses over the cocktail menu at his speakeasy-style lounge inside the East Village hot dog joint Crif Dogs. *113 Saint Marks Pl., Manhattan; 212.614.0386.*

PEGU CLUB
Audrey Saunders, a leader of the vintage-cocktail movement, co-owns this spot. Drinks arrive with dropper bottles of bitters. *77 W. Houston St., Manhattan; 212.473.7348.*

PRIME MEATS
Frank Castronovo and Frank Falcinelli's homage to early Brooklyn has a German-style barroom and an upstairs speakeasy. *465 Court St., Brooklyn; 718.254.0327.*

SILVER LINING
A live jazz quintet plays nightly at this Tribeca bar opened recently by three cocktail masters. *75 Murray St., Manhattan; 212.513.1234.*

THE TIPPLER
Tad Carducci and Paul Tanguay, the cocktail-consulting Tippling Bros., are behind this rustic tavern under Chelsea Market. *425 W. 15th St., Manhattan; 212.206.0000.*

PHILADELPHIA

THE FARMERS' CABINET
This restaurant and barroom is named for the 1800s newspaper believed to have first used the word "cocktail." *1113 Walnut St.; 215.923.1113; thefarmerscabinet.com.*

THE FRANKLIN MORTGAGE & INVESTMENT CO.
In a building that fronted the nation's largest alcohol-smuggling ring during Prohibition, this bar maintains a speakeasy feel. *112 S. 18th St.; 267.467.3277.*

THE RANSTEAD ROOM
Star bartender Sasha Petraske consulted on the drinks at this side-street lounge. *2013 Ranstead St.; no phone; elreyrestaurant.com.*

TEQUILAS RESTAURANT
David Suro-Piñera owns this elegant hacienda-style restaurant with Mexican-inspired cocktails and around 100 tequilas. *1602 Locust St.; 215.546.0181; tequilasphilly.com.*

WASHINGTON, DC AREA

COLUMBIA ROOM P.51
Derek Brown runs this quiet cocktail club inside The Passenger, a lively saloon overseen by his brother, Tom. *1021 Seventh St. NW, Washington, DC; 202.393.0220.*

THE GIBSON
This exclusive bar with a no-standing policy is all about well-crafted cocktails. The waitstaff flames twists tableside. *2009 14th St. NW, Washington, DC; 202.232.2156.*

PX
This chandelier-lit speakeasy is owned by Todd Thrasher (P.79) and the team behind the terrific Restaurant Eve. *728 King St., Alexandria, VA; 703.299.8384.*

TABARD INN
Cocktails like the vermouth-based Old Hickory, supposedly enjoyed by Andrew Jackson, are served at this bar in a 1920s inn. *1739 N St. NW, Washington, DC; 202.331.8528.*

GREAT LAKES & MIDWEST

CHICAGO

THE AVIARY P.44
Craig Schoettler's futuristic drinks are the draw at this bar inspired by molecular gastronomy. *955 W. Fulton Market; 312.226.0868; theaviary.com.*

BAR DEVILLE

Described by its owners as resembling a Parisian dive bar, Bar DeVille serves Manhattans and Margaritas as well as cans of cold PBR. *701 N. Damen Ave.; 312.929.2349; bardeville.com.*

THE BARRELHOUSE FLAT

Violet Hour alum Stephen Cole opened this homage to classic cocktails. Weekends, there's live ragtime music played on an upright piano. *2624 N. Lincoln Ave.; 773.857.0421; barrelhouseflat.com.*

THE DRAWING ROOM

Charles Joly is the head bartender at this subterranean restaurant and lounge. Guests can have their drinks prepared from a custom bar cart, accompanied by a cocktail history lesson. *937 N. Rush St.; 312.266.2694.*

SABLE KITCHEN & BAR P.144

Mike Ryan serves classics like his excellent Sazerac from this elegant gastrolounge's 40-foot-long bar. *505 N. State St.; 312.755.9704; sablechicago.com.*

THE VIOLET HOUR

Modeled after early-19th-century English clubs and French salons, this lounge introduced the New York–style classic-cocktails scene to Chicago. *1520 N. Damen Ave.; 773.252.1500; theviolethour.com.*

THE WHISTLER

While guests check out live music, film screenings and an art gallery, Paul McGee makes drinks like the Rittenhouse rye–based Arrigo Park. *2421 N. Milwaukee Ave.; 773.227.3530; whistlerchicago.com.*

MILWAUKEE

BRYANT'S COCKTAIL LOUNGE

Bryant's has been around since 1938, and the lounge looks as if time stopped in 1976. Customers can order by spirit, flavor, strength, texture or even color. *1579 S. Ninth St.; 414.383.2620; bryantscocktaillounge.com.*

DISTIL

Known for its 120-plus bourbons and ryes, Distil has drinks like a bourbon Old-Fashioned infused with Wisconsin's famous Nueske's bacon. *722 N. Milwaukee St.; 414.220.9411; distilmilwaukee.com.*

MADISON, WI

MADURO

This cigar- and pipe-friendly lounge has a rotating selection of stogies and a vast spirits list focusing on Scotch and bourbon. *117 E. Main St.; 608.294.9371.*

MERCHANT

At this farm-to-table restaurant, bartenders serve up elegantly presented classics. *121 S. Pinckney St.; 608.259.9799.*

NOSTRANO

Nostrano's barkeeps turn out barrel-aged Manhattans and inventions like Winter Tonic, made with Chicago-area North Shore #6 gin. *111 S. Hamilton St.; 608.395.3295.*

MINNEAPOLIS

BRADSTREET CRAFTSHOUSE

A velvet curtain hides a private "parlour room" at this bar in Graves 601 Hotel. Toby Maloney created the drink menu. *601 First Ave. N.; 612.312.1821; bradstreetcraftshouse.com.*

CAFE MAUDE

This bistro and bar serves a dozen "breakfast cocktails," including a riff on the classic Bronx topped with bitter orange foam. *5411 Penn Ave. S.; 612.822.5411; cafemaude.com.*

ST. LOUIS

MONARCH

New Orleans inspires both the food and the cocktails here. Around the holidays, bartenders whip up Sazerac-like Spicy Nutcrackers. *7401 Manchester Rd.; 314.644.3995; monarchrestaurant.com.*

ST. LOUIS CONTINUED

SANCTUARIA
At this tapas bar hung with Latino artwork, Matt Seiter serves cocktails on tap and innovations like the bourbon-based 47th Ward, sweetened with hibiscus syrup. *4198 Manchester Ave.; 314.535.9700;* sanctuariastl.com.

TASTE
Ted Kilgore organizes his drink menu by flavor: Hell's Bells (gin, Pimm's, lemon juice and smoked red bell peppers) falls under "Tart, Spiced, Savory." *4584 Laclede Ave.; 314.361.1200;* tastebarstl.com.

KANSAS CITY, MO

MANIFESTO P.110
This speakeasy-style bar evokes the '20s, but Ryan Maybee serves modern cocktails, too, like Smokin' Choke, with house-smoked bourbon. *1924 Main St.; 816.536.1325.*

THE RIEGER HOTEL GRILL & EXCHANGE
Another Ryan Maybee venture, this spot in a refurbished 1915 hotel serves house-made sodas from old-school seltzer dispensers. *1924 Main St.; 816.471.2177;* theriegerkc.com.

SOUTH

NASHVILLE

CITY HOUSE
This thin-crust pizza joint has terrific sparkling and dessert cocktails, plus a bar-food menu with a section called "Pork Snacks." *1222 Fourth Ave. N.; 615.736.5838.*

MERCHANTS
Merchants' first floor resembles a 1940s drugstore diner and serves Tennessee twists on classics, like peach rum Mojitos. *401 Broadway; 615.254.1892;* merchants restaurant.com.

THE PATTERSON HOUSE
Übermixologist Toby Maloney is behind the drink menu at this bar named for the Tennessee governor who vetoed the return of statewide Prohibition in 1909. *1711 Division St.; 615.636.7724;* thepattersonnashville.com.

ATLANTA AREA

H. HARPER STATION
Mixologist Jerry Slater transformed an old rail depot into a destination for drinks like The Alchemist (malt whiskey and oloroso sherry mixed with apple butter and allspice dram). *904 Memorial Dr. SE, Atlanta; 678.732.0415;* hharperstation.com.

HOLEMAN & FINCH PUBLIC HOUSE P.119
At this excellent gastropub, mixologist Greg Best uses sorghum to sweeten drinks such as the bourbon-based Copper and Cane. *2277 Peachtree Rd., Atlanta; 404.948.1175;* holeman-finch.com.

LEON'S FULL SERVICE P.168
Not only does this restaurant in a former filling station make its own liqueurs and bitters, it has bar snacks worth traveling for (local bacon with homemade peanut butter) and a bocce court. *131 E. Ponce de Leon Ave., Decatur; 404.687.0500;* leonsfullservice.com.

MIAMI & MIAMI BEACH

LIVING ROOM BAR
The mixologists at this luxe lounge in the W Hotel use unusual ingredients like Sriracha, roast herbs for cocktails with blowtorches and top drinks with flavored foams. *2201 Collins Ave., Miami Beach; 305.938.3000;* wsouthbeach.com.

SRA. MARTINEZ
Chorizo bitters and syrups infused with *ají amarillo* chiles flavor the Latin-inspired drinks at chef Michelle Bernstein's restaurant. *4000 NE Second Ave., Miami; 305.573.5474;* sramartinez.com.

NEW ORLEANS

ARNAUD'S FRENCH 75 BAR P.48
Chris Hannah mans the bar at this dapper, cigar-friendly spot inside Arnaud's, one of New Orleans's oldest and most venerated restaurants. *813 Bienville St.; 504.523.5433;* arnaudsrestaurant.com.

CURE P.133
Owner Kirk Estopinal and bartender Rhiannon Enlil use droppers to add house-made tinctures to cocktails. The Scotch-based Vixen's Heart is flavored with a salt tincture and smoked grapefruit oil. *4905 Freret St.; 504.302.2357;* curenola.com.

TEXAS

ANVIL BAR & REFUGE
Classic-cocktail devotee Bobby Heugel serves flips, brambles, bucks and sours and hosts monthly themed cocktail classes at this bar in an old Bridgestone-Firestone tire shop. *1424 Westheimer Rd., Houston; 713.523.1622;* anvilhouston.com.

BAR CONGRESS
Chicken-fried olives and drinks like the árbol chile–spiked Mestizo (made with sotol, a tequila-like spirit that's new to the US) draw cocktail geeks to this tiny downtown bar. *200 Congress Ave., Austin; 512.827.2760;* congressaustin.com/bar-congress.

THE ESQUIRE TAVERN
Founded in 1933 (the year Prohibition ended), this old-school hangout has a long wooden bar, tin ceilings and excellent bar snacks (fried pickles, boiled peanuts). *155 E. Commerce St., San Antonio; 210.222.2521;* esquiretavern-sa.com.

MARQUEE GRILL & BAR
At *Top Chef* contestant Tre Wilcox's new restaurant, diners sip cocktails on the upstairs balcony, which also serves as the marquee for the Village Theater downstairs. *32 Highland Park Village, Dallas; 214.522.6035;* marqueegrill.com.

SOUTHWEST

DENVER/BOULDER/ASPEN

THE BITTER BAR
Mark Stoddard and his crew make some of Boulder's best pre-Prohibition drinks at this hidden cocktail and dessert lounge. *835 Walnut St., Boulder; 303.442.3050;* thebitterbar.com.

JIMMY'S
This Aspen institution has more than 100 tequilas and mezcals, serves terrific Margaritas and hosts legendary Latin-dance parties. *205 S. Mill St., Aspen; 970.925.6020.*

OAK AT FOURTEENTH P.83
Frasca Food & Wine alums Bryan Dayton and Steven Redzikowski co-own this restaurant, where Dayton offers NA (nonalcoholic), LA (low-alcohol) and HA (high-alcohol) drinks. *1400 Pearl St., Boulder; 303.444.3622.*

WILLIAMS & GRAHAM P.71
Guests must pass through a door disguised as a bookcase to reach barman Sean Kenyon's speakeasy-style cocktail haven. *3160 Tejon St., Denver; 303.997.8886.*

LAS VEGAS

DOWNTOWN COCKTAIL ROOM
In a renovated wedding chapel marked by a tiny sign, this lounge offers half a dozen absinthes and classic drinks like the orgeat-sweetened Japanese Cocktail. *111 Las Vegas Blvd. S.; 702.880.3696.*

PARASOL DOWN P.65
Colorful upside-down parasols decorate the ceiling of this Wynn Las Vegas lounge; Patricia Richards created its excellent drink list. *3131 Las Vegas Blvd. S.; 702.770.7000.*

VESPER BAR
At this glittering lounge in the Cosmopolitan of Las Vegas, the knowledgeable bartenders improvise with ingredients like black salt. *3708 Las Vegas Blvd. S.; 702.698.7000.*

WEST COAST

SAN DIEGO

NOBLE EXPERIMENT P.116
Entry to this exclusive bar—via the burger joint Neighborhood—is granted by a text saying, "You're on the list." Sam Ross of NYC's Little Branch consulted on the drinks. 777 G St.; 619.888.4713; nobleexperimentsd.com.

PROHIBITION
Drinks are served in copper mugs and mason jars at this speakeasy-style bar with live jazz. 548 Fifth Ave.; 619.663.5485.

SALTBOX
At this gastrolounge, mixologist Erin Williams offers drinks like Off the Beet'en Path, with saffron-infused gin, yuzu, ginger and beet brine. 1047 Fifth Ave.; 619.515.3003.

LOS ANGELES AREA

BAR 1886
Cocktail veterans Aidan Demarest and Marcos Tello (P.163) opened this bar adjacent to the Raymond Restaurant. 1250 S. Fair Oaks Ave., Pasadena; 626.441.3136.

CAÑA RUM BAR
This tony Cuban-style spot charges first-time visitors $20, then donates the fees to charity. Try one of their three classic Daiquiris. 714 W. Olympic Blvd., Los Angeles; 213.745.7090.

COPA D'ORO P.26
Headed by Vincenzo Marianella, Copa d'Oro has a "be your own mixologist" option, which allows guests to concoct drinks with seasonal ingredients and top-notch spirits. 217 Broadway, Santa Monica; 310.576.3030; copadoro.com.

HARVARD & STONE
This rustic-industrial saloon from the duo behind La Descarga has a "test kitchen" bar, featuring a different spirit each month; American distillers are the focus. 5221 Hollywood Blvd., Los Angeles; 323.466.6063.

LA DESCARGA
This Old Havana–inspired rum bar serves vintage rum cocktails and hosts classes about the spirit in its "cigar room." 1159 N. Western Ave., Los Angeles; 323.466.1324.

RIVERA
Guests at John Rivera Sedlar's modern Latin restaurant can sample Julian Cox's seasonal tequila infusions, all on tap, as well as Rivera's private-label, extra-aged añejo. 1050 S. Flower St., Los Angeles; 213.749.1460.

SEVEN GRAND
Part Irish pub, part English hunting lodge, this hip lounge serves more than 300 whiskeys and Maker's Mark–dipped cigars. 515 W. Seventh St., Los Angeles; 213.614.0737.

THE SPARE ROOM P.147
Naomi Schimek's swank bar at the Hollywood Roosevelt hotel is modeled after an old-fashioned gentlemen's parlor. 7000 Hollywood Blvd., Los Angeles; 323.769.7296.

THE TASTING KITCHEN
At this restaurant, nearly everything (butchering, pickling, curing) is done in-house; bartenders pay the same attention to drinks. 1633 Abbot Kinney Blvd., Venice; 310.392.6644.

THE VARNISH P.103
A collaboration between cocktail magnates Sasha Petraske and Eric Alperin, The Varnish is entered through a secret door at Cole's, the famous French dip restaurant. 118 E. Sixth St., Los Angeles; 213.622.9999.

SAN FRANCISCO

15 ROMOLO
Bartenders at this 21st-century saloon whip up intriguing concoctions like a Bloody Mary spiced with whiskey barrel–aged smoked-pepper sauce. 15 Romolo Pl.; 415.398.1359.

THE ALEMBIC
At this gastropub, Daniel Hyatt offers a terrific list of "After-Dinner Libations" like Scotch and "Daytime" drinks like Mint Juleps. 1725 Haight St.; 415.666.0822.

BAR AGRICOLE P.128
Rhum agricole–lover Thad Vogler, who designed the Slanted Door's drink menu, co-owns this tavern. *355 11th St.; 415.355.9400;* baragricole.com.

BERETTA P.99
Ryan Fitzgerald mans the bar at this upscale pizzeria's late-night cocktail lounge. *1199 Valencia St.; 415.695.1199;* berettasf.com.

COMSTOCK SALOON P.150
Jonny Raglin and Jeff Hollinger run this 1900s-style bar serving period-appropriate cocktails and snacks like corn hominy fritters. *155 Columbus Ave.; 415.617.0071.*

JASPER'S CORNER TAP & KITCHEN
This gastropub has beer cocktails, Negronis on tap and a whole menu devoted to *poutine* (french fries topped with cheese curds and gravy). *401 Taylor St.; 415.775.7979.*

NOPA
The bartenders at this neighborhood restaurant use as many local ingredients as possible, including honey from their rooftop hives. *560 Divisadero; 415.864.8643;* nopasf.com.

RICKHOUSE
From the owners of Bourbon & Branch, Rickhouse specializes in whiskey and whiskey-based drinks such as the Rye Maple Fizz. *246 Kearny St.; 415.398.2827;* rickhousesf.com.

THE SLANTED DOOR P.122
Many of Erik Adkins's cocktails are designed to complement Charles Phan's modern Vietnamese menu. *1 Ferry Bldg.; 415.861.8032.*

SMUGGLER'S COVE P.92
Rum fanatic Martin Cate's bar offers 200 rums to members of its Rumbustion Society. Bartender Marco Dionysos uses the spirit in his Mai Tais and other great drinks. *650 Gough St.; 415.869.1900;* smugglerscovesf.com.

WILSON & WILSON
This reservations-only nook inside Bourbon & Branch offers a three-course prix fixe cocktail flight (an aperitif, a "main" drink and a digestif). *505 Jones St.; no phone;* thewilsonbar.com.

PORTLAND, OR

CLYDE COMMON
Jeffrey Morgenthaler oversees the rotating drink list at this industrial tavern adjacent to the Ace Hotel. Try their barrel-aged cocktails. *1014 SW Stark St.; 503.228.3333.*

KASK
From the team behind the restaurant Grüner, this bar features small-batch spirits from American distillers and local charcuterie. *1215 SW Alder St.; 503.241.7163.*

OVEN & SHAKER
Star bartender Ryan Magarian creates the drinks at his great new pizza-and-cocktails place. *1134 NW Everett St.; 503.241.1600.*

TEARDROP COCKTAIL LOUNGE P.156
Daniel Shoemaker and his fellow bartenders make their own tonic water and specialty liqueurs. *1015 NW Everett St.; 503.445.8109.*

THE WOODSMAN TAVERN
Duane Sorenson opened this new restaurant next door to his flagship Stumptown café. Evan Zimmerman oversees the bar. *4537 SE Division St.; 971.373.8264.*

SEATTLE

CANON: WHISKEY & BITTERS EMPORIUM P.58
The mahogany bar at Jamie Boudreau's new place was stained using three cases of Angostura bitters. *928 12th Ave.; 206.552.9755.*

ROB ROY P.137
Anu Apte's bar feels like a 1960s bachelor pad. It even has an eight-track tape player. *2332 Second Ave.; 206.956.8423.*

SAMBAR
Perhaps the smallest bar in Seattle (it seats 14), Sambar serves some of the best drinks in town. *425 NW Market St.; 206.781.4883.*

ZIG ZAG CAFÉ
At this Seattle institution, the bartenders mix forgotten drinks based on old cocktail recipes. *1501 Western Ave.; 206.625.1146.*

RECIPE INDEX

Page numbers in **bold** indicate photographs.

cocktails

party food

BARWARE GUIDE

cocktails

CONTENTS

P.4 *"Mitos" Champagne coupe by Arik Levy from Ameico,* accessories.ameico.com; *"Basso" Champagne saucer,* calvinklein.com; *"Circus" wallpaper,* cole-and-son.com.

FOREWORD

P.6 *"Optic" tumbler by Ciovere,* 401.864.4377.

GLASSWARE

P.8 [1] *"I Professionali" martini glass,* tableart online.com; [2] *"Madrid" glass by LSA from the Conran Shop,* elementsforhome.com; [3] *"Carat" glass by Lena Bergström,* orrefors. us; [4] *"Basso" wineglass,* calvinklein.com; [5] *"Wave" highball glass by Donna Karan,* lenox.com; [6] *"Patrician" Champagne cup by Lobmeyr,* neuegalerie.org; [7] *"Simple" pilsner glass by Deborah Ehrlich for Moss,* mossonline.com; [9] *"Simple" flute,* nouvel studio.com; [10] *fizz glass by Deborah Ehrlich,* erbutler.com; *"Sussex" wallpaper from Designers Guild,* designersguild.com.

HOME BAR TOOLS

P.10 [1] *"Diamond" ice pick,* [4] *premium julep strainer,* [6] *"AG" cobbler shaker,* [8] *"Baron" strainer and* [11] *"Yarai" mixing glass,* cocktailkingdom.com; [2] *bar spoon,* caskstore.com; [5] *"Chef sommelier" corkscrew by L'Atelier du Vin,* fitzsu.com; [7] *martini atomizer,* winestuff.com; [9] *citrus press by Norpro,* amazon.com; [10] *Boston shaker and* [12] *cocktail measure,* alessi-shop.com; [13] *grater,* us.microplane.com; [14] *PUG! muddler by Chris Gallagher from Mjölk,* store.mjolk.ca; [15] *strainer,* rosleusa.com.

party food

MIXOLOGISTS

ERIK ADKINS (P.122) manages the bar at the Slanted Door in San Francisco.

BRIDGET ALBERT (P.140) is the director of mixology for Southern Wine & Spirits of Illinois in Chicago.

ERIC ALPERIN (P.103) is a co-owner and bartender at The Varnish in Los Angeles.

ANU APTE (P.137) is the owner and drinks expert at Rob Roy in Seattle.

GREG BEST (P.119) is a co-owner and bartender at Atlanta's Holeman & Finch Public House and co-owner of H&F Bottle Shop, a spirits, wine and house-made-mixers store.

JACQUES BEZUIDENHOUT (P.114) is the master mixologist at San Francisco's Fifth Floor restaurant and lounge. He is also the chief beverage consultant for Kimpton Hotels and Restaurants.

JAMIE BOUDREAU (P.58) owns Canon: Whiskey and Bitters Emporium in Seattle.

DEREK BROWN (P.51) is a co-owner of the Columbia Room and The Passenger, both in Washington, DC.

JACKSON CANNON (P.87) is a co-owner of The Hawthorne, which recently opened in Boston's Hotel Commonwealth, and the bar director at the neighboring Eastern Standard and Island Creek Oyster Bar.

KATHY CASEY (P.74) is a chef, mixologist, author and restaurant consultant based in Seattle. Her online cocktail show, Kathy Casey's Liquid Kitchen, is on liquidkitchen.tv.

BRYAN DAYTON (P.83) is the co-owner and beverage director of Oak at Fourteenth in Boulder, CO.

JOHN DEBARY (P.61) tends the bar at PDT and Momofuku Ssäm Bar, both in New York City. He tested all the drink recipes for this book.

MARCO DIONYSOS (P.92) mixes drinks at Smuggler's Cove in San Francisco.

RHIANNON ENLIL (P.133) is a bartender at Cure in New Orleans.

RYAN FITZGERALD (P.99) is the director of spirits and cocktails at Beretta pizzeria and bar in San Francisco.

JOHN GERTSEN (P.160) helped create the bar program at Boston's No. 9 Park before collaborating with chef Barbara Lynch to open Drink, also in Boston, where he is the general manager.

CHRIS HANNAH (P.48) mans the bar at Arnaud's French 75 Bar in New Orleans.

SEAN KENYON (P.71) is the owner and barkeep at Williams & Graham in Denver and writes a weekly cocktail column for the Denver Westword, a community newspaper.

FRANCESCO LAFRANCONI (P.22) is the national director of mixology and spirits educator for Southern Wine & Spirits of America.

JOHN LERMAYER (P.55), formerly of the Florida Room at the Delano Hotel, created the cocktail menu for the new Blackbird Ordinary in Miami, where he also tends bar.

MILES MACQUARRIE (P.168) manages the bar at Leon's Full Service in Decatur, GA.

VINCENZO MARIANELLA (P.26) is the head bartender at Copa d'Oro in Santa Monica, CA. His beverage consulting business is called Mymixology.

LYNNETTE MARRERO (P.34) owns a cocktail catering and event planning company called Drinks at 6 in New York City.

RYAN MAYBEE (P.110) owns Manifesto and co-owns the Rieger Hotel Grill & Exchange, both in Kansas City, MO.

ANDREW POLLARD (P.96) develops drinks for Wirtz Beverage Nevada. He's based in Las Vegas.

LINDEN PRIDE (P.125) is the general manager of Saxon & Parole and director of operations for AvroKO Hospitality Group in New York City.

JONNY RAGLIN (P.150) is a co-founder and bartender at San Francisco's Comstock Saloon.

JULIE REINER (P.153) owns or co-owns several cocktail lounges in New York City: Lani Kai, Flatiron Lounge and the Pegu Club, all in Manhattan, and Clover Club in Brooklyn.

LYDIA REISSMUELLER (P.41) owns Tender Bar Cocktail Catering in Portland, OR.

PATRICIA RICHARDS (P.65) is the master mixologist for Wynn and Encore resorts in Las Vegas.

LEO ROBITSCHEK (P.68) manages the bar at Eleven Madison Park in New York City.

MIKE RYAN (P.144) is the head bartender at Sable Kitchen & Bar in Chicago.

NAOMI SCHIMEK (P.147) is the beverage director at the Spare Room in L.A.'s Hollywood Roosevelt hotel.

ANTHONY SCHMIDT (P.116) is owner and bartender at Noble Experiment in San Diego.

CRAIG SCHOETTLER (P.44) is the chef at The Aviary cocktail bar in Chicago.

FRANCIS SCHOTT (P.171) co-owns Catherine Lombardi and Stage Left restaurants, both in New Brunswick, NJ. He is also co-host and co-creator of the Restaurant Guys Radio podcast.

DANIEL SHOEMAKER (P.156) owns Teardrop Cocktail Lounge in Portland, OR.

JOAQUÍN SIMÓ (P.90) is a founding bartender at Death & Co. in New York City and a partner in Alchemy Consulting, a cocktail bar development company. He was a deputy editor of F&W Cocktails 2009 and 2010. His new bar, Pouring Ribbons, opens in New York in early 2012.

MARCOS TELLO (P.163) is the chief cocktail consultant at Killer Shrimp in Marina del Rey, CA, and founder of the Sporting Life cocktail guild.

TODD THRASHER (P.79) is a co-owner and bartender at Restaurant Eve, PX, the Majestic, Eamonn's a Dublin Chipper and Virtue Feed & Grain, all in Alexandria, VA.

THAD VOGLER (P.128) established the bar programs at the Slanted Door, Coco 500, the Presidio Social Club, Camino, Beretta and the Lounge at the Jardinière, all in San Francisco. He is a co-owner and bartender at Bar Agricole, also in San Francisco.

CHARLOTTE VOISEY (P.29) is a mixologist for William Grant & Sons, USA, and manages cocktail programs across the country.

DAMIAN WINDSOR (P.106) is a bartender at the Roger Room in Los Angeles and founder of For Medicinal Purposes, a cocktail bar consulting company.

DUSHAN ZARIC (P.38) is the head bartender and a co-owner of Employees Only in New York City.

THANK YOU

In addition to everyone who contributed recipes, the following people were indispensable in making this book possible: Greg Boehm, Paul and Victoria deBary, Simon Ford, Ryan Huber, Toby Maloney, Valerie Meehan, Michael Remaley and Brian Shebairo.

More books from

FOOD&WINE

Annual Cookbook
An entire year of FOOD & WINE recipes.

Best of the Best Cookbook Recipes
The best recipes from the 25 best cookbooks of the year.

Wine Guide
Pocket-size guide with more than 1,000 recommendations.

Available wherever books are sold, or call **800-284-4145**
or log on to **foodandwine.com/books**